The Mom Egg

The Mom Egg

LESSONS

2010 Vol. 8

Edited by

Marjorie Tesser

Half-Shell Press
NEW YORK

The Mom Egg

Editor - Marjorie Tesser

Founding Editor - Alana Ruben Free
Founding Publisher - Joy Rose & Mamapalooza

The Mom Egg, an annual collection of poetry, fiction, creative prose, and art, publishes work by mothers about everything, and by everyone about mothers and motherhood, and is engaged in promoting and celebrating the creative force of mother artists, and in expanding the opportunities for mothers, women, and artists.

Cover Image "All You Need to Know" by Orna Ben-Shoshan

With thanks to Sue Altman and Amanda Laycock - design/layout.

The Mom Egg 2010 Vol. 8 ©Half-Shell Press and Marjorie Tesser, 2010.
All rights reserved.

The Mom Egg is grateful for the assistance of the Council of Literary Magazines and Presses, the New York State Council on the Arts, a state agency, and The Motherhood Foundation.

ISBN# 1451585535
EAN-13 9781451585537

Website: **http://themomegg.com**

Contact: **themomegg@gmail.com**

Half-Shell Press
New York

TABLE OF CONTENTS

LANGUAGE CLASS

(written on Qualla Boundary; for C.M.)

Little by little
we are reclaiming the words
Just as the land was once large,
so, too, our voice
Some words lost on the Trail
have been found
They lived hidden in baskets,
in pockets, in the very tassels of corn
(*Selu, Selu)*
Now the words live again
See? When I say *nogwo* it is now,
both the now of then and the now
of not yet
The words work secret medicine
and strong, forming us
from the inside out
Language is our Magic Lake--
we walk in limping with loss
and emerge wholly ourselves
When Cecilia speaks
she bears with her
the future of these sounds
Listen: her voice is soft, but sure

Kimberly L. Becker

BAH

'Later, I say, picking up my hat.
Back in an hour!
Off to the grocery!
Time to go home.
See you tomorrow.

Bah, he says, waving goodbye
with his baby hand. He
can't tell us how
he knew. Was it the hat?
the grocery bag? The car-
keys? Or a certain
goodbye stance, a goodbye
intonation he's absorbed
an unmistakable
gestalt. *Bah*, he says today.
Have a good one,
coming down the track.

Marian Kaplun Shapiro

WAYS TO SAY THE WORLD

1.
Clara claimed the world,
like Eve did in Eden, by naming it.

At 2, having developed a fondness for k,
she crunched duck and ticket
like spoonfuls of Cheerios.
Then it was z. She sang zinnia and pansy
into gardens abuzz with bees.
Large with self, she dragged mine
through the house like a deed of ownership.

When Cecelia spoke, we saw the world
through clean windows.

2.
When 5-year-old Faith
finally spoke, the world
we had names for disappeared.
We reminded each other of Einstein
who didn't speak until he was past 5.

Now we search her water-green eyes for meaning.
We wade into opaque seas.

Sometimes we find coral.

Judith Tate O'Brien

ACROBATIC ALPHABET

Anytime Mother read the musical sound
Bombarded me as if hula hoops had
Crashed toward an acrobat who
Did not remember how to dive through
Each bright round as it shivered by.

Finding the center was hard. I
Got little from a plot, always
Hated the handsome knight's forays
In to castles so nicely sinister,
Just wanted to be a jester
Knotting myself into each letter.

"Look 'L' sits on 'h,' no, better,
Meek "A" caresses her bent knees,
Naughty 'S's' hiss while 'V's' tease…"

"Oh, sit down!" (Mother could be mean.)
"Pay attention. If you never
Quit squirming, how will you learn to
Read?"
    Sweaty, red-faced, I never
Said to her that someday I'd
Turn the old words inside out to find
Untold stuff. I'd unbind her
Voice from tales of glory
Wrench my body from her mind,
Xerox consonants, bend to rhyme.
Yield to vowels, be the humble
Zany free to move and make trouble.

Katherine Swett

A GOURMET'S LINGUISTIC ANALYSIS OF CULTURE

(apologies to Joseph Campbell)

EAT is a three-letter word
short and sweet
what we do with our food
how we grow as in
"you are what you eat"

TEAT is a four-letter word
from whence we draw sustenance
our first food
our mother's gift

MEAT is the hunter's diet
notice the force of it
MMEEEE   TTTT
strong like the hunters
our ancestors
each his own priest
seeking his own vision
his own meat

Now listen to WHEAT
soft and whiney
overlong
overprocessed
look at planter cultures
full of human sacrifice
established priesthoods

Beware the vegetarians, my friends
their history is not good

Helen Ruggieri

THE NORTH WIND, POETRY, AND PIMENTOS

(a poetry lesson in a fourth grade classroom at
Nakajima Elementary School, Oita, Japan)

Cha-wan o mi-mi ni a-te-ru to
If you hold a bowl close to your ear...
Hyu, hyu, hyu to o-to ga su-ru
you'll hear a breezy sound.
Like a ferris wheel
Gu-ru,-gu-ru
that circles round
and round.

Cha-wan no naka day,
I hear a teacher from the next room say.
As the teacher in the room I'm in
draws chalk circles in pink
like roses
around the ways that poems
and prose
are different.

A child in red
stands up to say:
*This poem is full
of circle play.*
While another points out
that there are no quotation marks
in poems.

Poems say what the writer wants to convey.
And in them,
un-like in a *bunsho* (composition),
expressing your opinion is
O.K.
Na-ni o so-zo shi-ta?
I hear the other teacher ask.

As the teacher in this class sniffs
the students' hair
and skin
she wiggles her fingers,
says *Ja…*
and takes out
a Pi-men-to.

Pi-man?
the children say at once.
Yes! She passes
pi-mans out to all.
Green peppers

are now being handled by excited hands.
I smile
at how poetry
transforms the PTA
into an un-expected wind today.
It wafts into
my consciousness.
I hold a vessel to my ear
and hear
a breezy sound.

Joanne G. Yoshida

LEARNING THE HARD WAY

I feel for the door-to-door evangelists,
the Jehovah's Witnesses, women in long skirts
and blue-gray sweaters, and the pairs
of handsome, clean-cut Mormon boys,
one always more shy than the other, holding
a stack of books and a bicycle helmet
under one arm. They are eager and
lovely, and even I don't invite them in.

My mother did when I was a child, because
she too felt called to witness. The seventh-day.
The second coming. Everything that made us
strange. She took out her Bible, its leather cover
worn as a pair of work gloves, and listened
to them expound their faith in the kind of earnest voices
movie actors reserve for speeches like, Please believe
me: an asteroid is on a collision course
with Earth. Her response was apologetic,
almost embarrassed; for every verse they quoted,

she knew two. I recognized the doubt soaking in,
the frustration. Still, they squared their shoulders.
No one wants to fall for the smooth sales pitch,
the telemarketer's call, the good news of the pamphlet
the glassy-eyed woman's hand. Whatever truth
there is, we want to find it for ourselves
like the ultimate rummage sale bargain.
Believe me, you can't tell us anything.

Amy Watkins

Ira Joel Haber

BABY BROTHER

He sat on the curb.
Baby Sister, he called out.
Talk to me
Please.
I leaned up on a tree.
His skinny black leather legs
were poised like knitting needles,
stars and demons sprinkled his arms.
You look like Nancy Spungeon he said,
but in a good way, you're prettier and nicer.
Bad luck plagued him.
Every time he hit someone, he got arrested;
his older sister refused his phone calls,
he wanted my advice, he knew I could help -
How could he make up with his sister?
She's his heart, the only one who cared.
I posed a question:
When you call her, do you ask for money?
Yeah, he said, *I need airfare,*
I gotta go to Seattle.
If you want to make up with your sister
I said, *call her and don't ask for money.*
He became impatient.
I can't do that, I gotta go to Seattle.
We said good-bye quite nicely.
I saw him again the next day.
He looked at me blankly,
but as I passed, I heard his voice
Bye Little Sister,
Love you, Nancy...

Puma Perl

A LESSON WE WERE NOT LIKELY TO FORGET

Dust blew up from the dirt road
as my mother braked the red Nash to a stop.
She walked to the rear of the car and
took a shovel out of the rounded trunk.
"Stay put, kids," she yelled,
not bothering to look back at us,
raising the shovel over a rattlesnake
coiled in the road. She swung the shovel down
on the snake and chopped off its head with
one quick motion that flipped it in the air
into a fence where it stuck in the barbed wire, fangs gaping.
She got back in the car and looked at herself
in the rearview mirror, puckering her lips up
to reapply a dash of red. She pulled hard on the gear shift,
started the car, and backed over the headless horror.
"Kids, don't ever try to be friendly with a rattler," she said.

Laurie Billman

ON SHAVU'OT

My grandchild asks what Jewish people believe in.
Her parents giving me that wide-eye look that signals
"HELP".   I jump in and bumble my way through
Sunday School platitudes: love, kindness, respect, etc.
Each one elicits a jaded silence from the kid.

I suspect I'm losing ground but can only think of
Pain, prejudice, persecution —
Not what I want to tell a five-year-old who still finds
Scary moments in *Winnie-The-Pooh*.
"C'mon," she says. "Like in the scroll, the *Torah*."

Now that I've led her to the place where my roots
Lie tangled within a borrowed name,
Can I confess I don't remember,
Maybe never even knew? Undone,
I tell my son to look for an answer on the Web.

Rosalie Calabrese

LESSON

Ten years old, visiting Manhattan
with mother, I spot a homeless man slumped
against a pigeon stained wall; head tilted
sideways, mouth open like wound. I turn
to stare as we pass. Snow begins to fall,
mother says it's from heaven. I envision
him covered, as if he were an old rug
tossed to the street. Mother pauses. I pull
her coat, ask why we're not stopping the way
we did for the stray dog we once carried
from the road. She takes my hand, hurries
me along, orders me to look the other
way. I have learned how to abandon.
And snow has nothing to do with heaven.

Ellen Saunders

CHARITY

My mother's voice curled
like a tin cup shaking a single coin
when she remembered the alley singers
of her youth in the Great Depression.

Their sonorous voices soared
through curtains of faded laundry,
releasing a spray of pigeons
and rising to the clouded panes

of her window. With an outstretched
hand she clutched a handkerchief
bundling tarnished change, dropping
the gift to the minstrel below

whose poverty cried more loudly
than her own. "There's always something
you can give," she told me.
I'll cherish those words as long as I live.

Mindy Kronenberg

SITTING IN MUD

There is a picture of us together, age two and five, maybe— Diana in a red gingham dress with puff sleeves, me in a pair of blue shorts and nothing on top. Beneath it in the photo album is my mother's crisp, looping handwriting: *Diana squealed, 'Ooh, I'm sitting in mud!'*

In the photo, I am standing, one elbow raised high, hand reaching down my back as if I'm holding a back scrubber, while the other hand is raised, palm facing the camera, mud dripping down my forearm, streaked on my legs, caked in my wet hair. Diana is squatting, the hem of her dress brown and wet, her nose scrunched up, a deranged, muddy grin spreading her mouth wide.

I thank my mother for this, and so many other days in the garden: examining snails with a magnifying glass, collecting rain in soup pans, climbing the old avocado tree and picking the little green fruits before they were ripe, just so we could carry them in our pockets and stroke their rough skins. Nature was magnificent to her, and therefore to us— the hummingbirds and butterflies, but also the spiders and potato bugs, the stink mushrooms that sprouted from the lawn after a rain, and the aphids that clung to the underside of leaves, their tiny green bodies camouflaged against the plant they fed on.

Forget god; this was a miracle: the way the little brown seeds we planted in spring became thin, sweet carrots, the way the beams of our flashlights shone back at us from the branches of the plum tree, reflected in the eyes of a baby raccoon.

The other day, I listened as my mother described to a group of friends a memory from her own childhood. "My mother would take me into the garden and show me snails," she said, "their little feelers, their delicate shells, and they were so wonderful and precious. And then one day a neighbor boy came over and when he saw a snail on the ground he said, 'Ooh, a snail!' Squish. And he stomped on it. In that moment, I thought: There are two kinds of people in this world. There are those who respect and love the little things in nature, and those who want to squish them."

These days I see young mothers everywhere; jogging with their babies in high-tech strollers, shopping at Trader Joe's with an infant in the shopping cart. I see mothers at the park with their children, and I always watch to see what happens when the kid goes to climb a tree, or examine a piece of trash, or eat a handful of sand, or whatever a child does to learn about the world. Sometimes I can almost taste the sand in my mouth, earthy, cool, gritty, before that young mother is snatching the little hand away and repeating that high-pitched mantra: "Nonononono," she'll say. "Don't do that. Icky. Dirty. Bad."

When I was in college I took a class called The American Forest, taught by a professor of art history and a professor of environmental science. I loved it. We studied the Hudson River School and forest succession, Arts and Crafts architecture and paper mills. I remember an etching of Jamestown or one of the early colonies: an orderly grouping of roads and buildings, and a dark forest closing it in on all sides: thick, black, threatening, impenetrable.

I am the child with a handful of sand and my eye on the forest at the end of the road, yearning to go explore, push past those branches, find out what lies beyond the safety of my tiny universe.

I like to picture a future in which I am a carefree young mother, hair loose, bosom full of milk, bare feet on the sun warmed earth and small children playing in the grass, coming to me with grasshoppers cupped in their hands, and leading me to the place under the hedge where they've made mud pies. I want to be like my own mother, to grab a camera and capture my babies squatting in the mud, not noticing that they're soiling their hand-me-down dresses. I want to show them daddy-long-legs and anthills, and take them for walks on dusty trails, and let them splash in tide pools. And if they fall down and scrape their knees, or get stung by bees, or get salt water in their eyes, I want to kiss them and say, "That's life, baby. Isn't it grand?"

Elizabeth Schwyzer

Markham Place was the closest mall to our house—you turned left at the corner of Cliffwood Road and kept going along Don Mills until you hit Steeles, and it was right there: a flat, faceless building, flat as everything along the road before it, except for the giant Sears entrance that towered as high as the senior citizen's home across the street where Gramma lived. At Markham Place, Mom and Papa developed their pictures and played Lotto, and Chi Chi bought food at the Miracle Mart. If I went to Miracle Mart with Mom and Chi Chi together, I got to sit in the shopping cart. If it was a trip with just Chi Chi, she said that five-year olds were too old to ride around like babies.

We went to Markham Place every Monday, when I had piano lessons in the upstairs. Either we could enter through Sears and walk through the toy section on the first floor, then take the escalator to the second, or we could enter the main mall and pass through a secret door next to the Yamaha store that led up a dirty, grey stairwell to the second floor. At one end of a hall that was carpeted and lined with offices were the music lesson studios. Hardly anyone knew about this part but us!

In the waiting room, Mom, Chi Chi, and I sat while we waited for our lessons. At 7:58 p.m., two Asian women with permed hair came out of separate piano rooms at the same time, leading out their 7:30 students and waving Mom and me toward them. Mom had lessons with Mrs. Yu, the taller one, and I had lessons with Mrs. Yun, the shorter one. Chi Chi sat in the waiting room and read her Hakka book.
Mrs. Yun told me I was one of the youngest students she'd ever had. She didn't want to take me at first because she didn't think I knew the alphabet.

As calm as she always was, Mom insisted on our first day that I was old enough. "Lily has known her alphabet since she was one and half! She can handle it." I wasn't even sure what she was committing me to at that point. "She will be fine!"

On other nights of the week, my bedtime was at eight, so sometimes I'd yawn during the lesson. Every few weeks, Mrs. Yun would close the piano lid, rest my head in her lap, and let me sleep.

Right after our lessons, I'd try to prolong our trip at Markham Place for as long as possible. We went to Grand and Toy so I could look at stickers, we went to Miracle Mart so Chi Chi could buy some broccoli, we went to the Lotto stand so Mom could play her Quick Picks.

Even if we climbed to the second floor through the secret doors on the way in, we always exited through Sears. Every other week, for several weeks, Mom let me buy a new Winnie the Pooh toy. We bought Winnie the first week we saw the display. But Mom, understanding the need for toy bears to have friends, knew that I would want the others as well. A couple of weeks later we bought Eeyore, then a couple of weeks later Tigger. Soon I also possessed Kanga, with Roo in her pouch.

One Monday night, Mom couldn't come to her piano lesson because she had to work late, so Papa took me instead. Papa didn't need anything at Miracle Mart and had already played Lotto, so we headed straight to the parking lot. As usual, we walked out through Sears, and though I wanted to slow down at the toy section, I didn't actually want to say anything about it. I didn't think Papa would get it. He and Mom were always yelling about money and Chi Chi told me it was because I was spoiled. He didn't see me looking over at the familiar stuffed toys. I didn't have Owl yet.

"MANING GEY COYSIM LOY GEY!" he shouted in the middle of bright walkway in Sears, grabbing my hand and lifting it with his. He shouted the words whenever he wanted me to squeal back, "Papa gey!" and run into his arms, one of the few Hakka call and responses we continued to maintain. I'd forgotten the rest of my Hakka by the time I was three.

I didn't say anything this time, though. Papa was so loud. There were so many people inside Sears who turned their heads when he shouted. I didn't even want Owl, I just wanted Papa to know that I wanted it, that that was what we did on Mondays after piano, that it was one night when Chi Chi didn't make me go to bed so early, because I had a secret place in the upstairs of Markham Place where I did important lessons with Mom that the people in the downstairs didn't know about. Mom knew what was supposed to happen on Mondays.

That night, as I was trying to pretend I was asleep, Chi Chi asked me why I was crying.

Veronica Liu

A USEFUL MAN

My mother's boyfriend was not good
at a lot of things.

Like the time mom left
on that trip to Chicago.
He didn't know to hold my hand
when her plane took off. Or that I
thought she might not come back.

But when I choked at
the dinner table,
when the meat bone
wedged in my throat,
he knew to hold me
upside down and swing
me from my feet
like the primate that I was.

Eyeballs in the eat-in kitchen
looking at linoleum,
I was slapped like
a baby. And the bone fell out.
And I was breathing again.

Back in front of our plates
he seemed, suddenly, capable.

Theta Pavis

SWALLOWED

My father used to paint
but I only saw him hold
a canvas once, to make
a warning sign.

He brushed fat letters
in thick blue paint: "Dock
Unsafe. Keep Off."

The next day he walked
past the sign and had me
follow him, both of us
holding a fishing rod. I watched
the weather-worn grey planks
under my feet.

Over the water we
went, past the sinking
middle section, which
looked like the collapsed
lung of an old whale.

We sat with our
feet dangling, lake water
beneath us, swallows darting
in and out from under
the dock, tending nests in
their sinking ship of a home.

But on the way back
the wood cracked, swallowing
me up to my midriff. A rusty
nail slashing its way
along my thigh, holding me fast.

I could see the cattails
waving their fuzzy heads at
me from the shoreline.

The great beast holding me
in its jaws, laughing at my
father who couldn't
follow his own advice.

Theta Pavis

CATALPA

My father. This is who he is: He is a man who grumbles all autumn at the catalpa tree that shades our side porch. The long, dry, weapon-like pods fall as if they were calculating an insult to his sensibilities, conspiring to keep him raking all spring. Cursing them for knowing how to escape the tines of his rake, he says, Not like leaves, which know how to give themselves up into his swift, harried movements. No, he says, these damn pods slip right through, like they know. He carts bushel after bushel to the back of the property. The next day a wind drops more, pushing some end-first into a lawn that is soft from recent snowmelt. The pod shells stand erect, and he goes about bending and pulling at them as if he were pulling at Excalibur, while my mother watches and shakes her head and smiles, knowing he will come in after an hour or so to complain over lunch. He is a man who sighs deeply when the sweet-smelling flowers start to quit their hold, drift down like a heavy snow, wither, and stick to the banisters and porch floorboards, leaving sepia shadows behind when he attempts to brush them off the white paint. And then the sugary droplets appear, sticky residue from the aphids that feed off the catalpa flowers, and he is there again, scrubbing and cursing at the mildew that erupts and spreads, like black crystals expanding, in the sap that is tacky hard.

My father. This is who he is not: He is not a man to pass by the porch's windows and ignore the catalpa after a summer downpour, when the large, elephantine leaves catch and hold the morning's hard rain, and the sky clears, and the sun comes out bringing with it a breeze, which knocks the rain off the leaves and sends the water spilling, so that it looks like it is raining liquid sunshine only under the catalpa, not anywhere else on Earth.

Tara Masih

POET

I pressed Clara's flowers
in the unabridged dictionary
years ago
in the pink and yellow times
and have just again found them
in the press of words.

She danced on a luminous stage
in pale pink slippers,
youngishly tossing our hearts,
and afterwards her grandparents gave her
yellow carnations,
which she has forgotten.

This is what I do:
I close and open the book.
It is a slow career,
but I do it: I press and then look
to see
what holds.

Mary Harter Mitchell

E.R.   Ellen Rix

Ira Joel Haber

fluff bunny

for Isabel Gibbs

> This poem was made by a mother noting down one colour
> every hour for 24 hours during one day of her pregnancy.
> She noted down a colour only when she was thinking of her
> baby. Colours have been substituted for words.

velvet velvet vellum skin
vellum skin pores velvet in
magenta pores vellum skin
sun velvet larks velvet
brink velvet light brink
sun velvet opens blink brink
light skin velvet in

honey honey drop orange
drop orange fields honey like
magenta fields drop orange
sunny honey hum honey
fur honey light fur
sunny honey buzz cup fur
light orange honey like

treacle treacle fluff bunny
fluff bunny fox treacle or
magenta fox fluff bunny
kiss treacle lip treacle
flip treacle fluff kiss
kiss treacle rush brush flip
light bunny treacle or

home home feels safe
feels safe warm home her
magenta warm feels safe
at home lips home
fold home light fold
at home encircle ever fold
light safe home her

ej burnett

FORTUNES

A friend in the process of adopting a baby from Vietnam came to visit last week. We discussed how getting from idea — let's adopt a baby — to baby sets in motion an involved process. I'm starting to appreciate that what's most transformative about this process is just beginning to unfold. With any baby, some of the gifts are complicated; with an adoption, there's this added element to grasp: much unbelievably good fortune has come our way in the form of a baby entrusted to us.

Our daughter arrived just before the year of golden pig ended. This is especially auspicious, as the golden pig year comes round only once every sixty. She burst into the world minutes after the polls opened on the East Coast for Super Tuesday during an election year in which the Democrats are putting forth her female and biracial identity in their two leading candidates. More immediate and intimate than those promising harbingers, I was asked to be present at her birth. That her birth mother, Caroline, wanted her baby's adoptive mother to welcome her, too, was an incredible privilege.

Despite having birthed three children myself and attended a number of other births, I'll admit to experiencing a surreal remove as I watched this baby's dark shock of hair and purple-pink body emerge from her mother's body. The midwife asked whether anyone — grandmother, aunt or me — wanted to cut the umbilical cord. One thing I was instantly certain of, I did not want to be the person to sever that initial tether between life-giver and the baby she'd borne. Actually, no one did.

I glanced over to Caroline. She was crying a little. Did she feel regret? Relief? Disbelief? Was there anything I could do just then to help her? I stayed back while her mom and sister ventured toward her. Nurses attended to the baby. My arms hung beside me, empty. Where did this baby actually belong? Where she was going? The answers were Caroline's to answer. Resolute, she uttered the name we'd chosen for the baby.

The nurse asked who wanted to hold her. I pointed to her grandmother. After a few minutes, she handed the baby to me. With a head of jet-black hair and ruddy, reddish skin, small nose, thin lips, petite gently curved face, and compact body, the baby was beautiful. She was a feather. I was so completely awed by her: a blessing, a gift bestowed unto the world, a free agent, a person perfectly herself in that moment.

I felt selfish in wanting her. All I wanted was to keep holding her. I wanted her, as in I didn't want to let her go.

When you say adoption, most people compliment you upon being a good person for offering an unfortunate child a "better" life. It's a somewhat different story at my local Whole Foods, though. During a recent visit, three other women on the checkout line commented upon how tiny my baby was and asked pointedly (as in, you don't look postpartum) how I was feeling. I explained that the baby was adopted, so physically, I felt just fine. All three, it turned out, were also adoptive mothers. Like joining a club, this secret society's stories spill out. Members' reactions are uniformly almost polar opposite to all those people lauding you for altruism: these mothers describe themselves as the recipients of "better" — as in enriched, blessed, expanded, and deepened — lives. Already, I cannot count how many women who've both given birth to and adopted children have told me: "You love them the same," or "You love her, in a way, even more. She's a gift." So, I emailed my friend upon returning home from Whole Foods that day and counseled her to go there. "Like Pooh talking about the rain clouds," I wrote, "start saying words like adoption and Vietnam and I'm certain you'll receive plenty of information."

Our baby is four weeks old now. Her skin is a little darker and less ruddy, her hair still voluminous if a bit sparser, her dark gray eyes open more often and for longer periods, her face fuller, her body strong, compact, and rounding out. She remains perfectly herself. I remain selfish. I want to hold her. All I know is that I'm the one who's blessed, so much so that this baby makes my heart burst.

Sarah Werthan Buttenwieser

BIRTH

When the doc told me my eggs were old
I went to my Buddhist altar
chanted to the universe
        to release this child
    from some faraway galaxy
            where goofball boys spring up from trampolines
                            of desire.
After death
miscarriages not of justice I can tell you
        two times the child inside died
    since my eggs were old, I was many times told.

Relenting
from some distant deep of memory
        finally forming
                this missing aching part of myself
He is.
His birth *a sleep*
            and a forgetting.

Lisa Williams

WARRIOR MOM

> "Women are strong, strong, terribly strong. We don't know how strong we are until we're pushing out our babies. We are often treated like babies when we should be in training, like acolytes, novices to the high priestesshood, like serious applicants for the space program."
> --Louise Erdrich, *The Blue Jay's Dance*

I am a warrior mom and I have been chosen for my children.

There is no other mother on the planet who is raising children exactly like mine, or with my special brand of mothering. This is MY beautiful mess. Every situation, every public meltdown, every parent-teacher conference, every lesson I learn as I ignore the stares, murmurs and judging glances of strangers – or of my own mother -- is unique to MY children, MY circumstances, MY precious chaos. I am in perpetual training with a constantly changing playing field but my purpose is clear. There is not only a method to my madness, there is task at hand that I have taken on with a vengeance – a vengeance like no other, like only a mother can muster.

Last year, I was the closest I'd ever been – and ever want to be -- to losing one of my children. I watched, horrified and helpless, as my beautiful, creative and sweet child moved farther and farther away from me, from our family, from all the joys in his life, into a dark, emotional abyss full of anxiety and fear. He stopped touching his toys. Objects throughout our home and school became "toxic." He refused to touch pencils, papers, books, doorknobs and even certain sections of the floor. His hands were chafed and bleeding from constant washing. Our lives were thrust into a whirlwind of doctors and therapists to combat a bizarre condition that was as cruel as it was insidious.

The warrior mom inside me was awakened the day my son was diagnosed with severe obsessive compulsive disorder. I knew that if I allowed myself to succumb to the overwhelming uncertainty and terror that engulfed me, my son would be lost. I also knew that no one could or would advocate for my son like I could. No one knows my son the way I do and I was prepared to fight like I had never done before.

I planned, organized, prepared and strategized. I read, researched and diligently followed up with a small army of specialists, doctors and teachers to keep them on task and focused on helping my son.
I insisted that he attend classes during his recovery, demanded access

to the school for therapy sessions, and initiated the necessary meetings and paperwork to get him immediate accommodations and support in the classroom. The day he returned to school, I sat in their main office the entire day to appease the worried and unprepared staff. Alas, they were not trained to handle a child who was suffering like mine, but that was not my problem. Like me, they had to rise above and beyond, because I would accept no less. Miraculously, I never lost my cool. There were many moments when I wanted to scream at everyone like a banshee. But I also knew that the diplomatic, politically correct mother generally wins out over the psycho-mother and I acted accordingly.

I began to keep a daily log of progress, teacher updates and doctors' reports. I began working with his therapist, side by side, to ensure that what he learned during his sessions, I could continue with him at home. And I made it clear – quite clear – to everyone involved, that when it came to my son, I would do everything and anything in my power to get him back. I would write every letter, make every call, attend every school meeting, make every appointment, read every book and join every organization to support me in the job of supporting him. In the end, I got my son back because I fought for him, and by example, I taught him how to fight for himself.

I learned my greatest lessons as a mother that year. I learned that every single day is to be cherished for its simple pleasures. I learned that my greatest goal as a mother is to ensure that my children learn to fight, as I have, for every opportunity to live the fullest, most fulfilling and happiest lives possible. I also learned that I possess an inner strength and determination as a mother that cannot be stopped.

I am a warrior mom and I have been chosen for my children.

Luz Celenia

THE PURPOSE OF US

We have two young children.
We don't get much sleep.

Two o'clock, four o'clock, six o'clock, eight –
these are the times we get up at night.

It's very glamorous. Wild hours,
bleary eyes, drunk with tiredness

we trudge on, cleverness gone,
energy distilled down

to one purpose: the kids
must not get sick or sad.

We don't need to
eat in restaurants

or have
any fun –

just
that.

Jessy Randall

THE BEAUTY OF BOREDOM

Boredom in grey sweatpants
shuffles in, hair like dislodged
couch springs. The girl hasn't
a good thing to say for herself
so let me spring to her aid. The beauty
of boredom is the lackluster way
she invites in randomness. One minute

you're mindlessly balling socks,
glancing every five seconds
at the clock; the next, you've hit on
an bizarre plot twist that makes
your novel murderously plausible.
Or maybe it's the too long unscrubbed
bathtub that you're hunched over

when suddenly the hunch you had
about a new kind of brush work
rushes up from the Comet like a meteor.
Occupy yourself with the blandest
of tasks, and your eyes turn inward,
voices start speaking, colors flow,
ideas and memories run over

your shoulders like shower water,
come at you like the center line,
make you cry like a cut onion.
Drudgery, repetition, sweat.
Inescapable, ridiculous to try.
The work gets done. You sleep well.
Brilliance is a by-product.

Greta Bolger

SOUND TRAVELS ON WATER

The smell of burnt toast is delicious.
Cold butter spreads smoother.
The first drag of coffee is sweeter.
Even small, insistent voices are pleasing.

Today, at least, hope travels
Like sound on water.
From my window I see the lake,
Drawn down for winter,
Yet still more
Than half full.

Kyle Potvin

SPECIES

on a line from Vijay Seshadri

If we have to have people, let them all be like you,
free of culture and costumes and trained appetite.
My sleek seal, my proud peacock, my precious gnu,
what do I want with people? I'd rather have you,
my sweet lynx, my gazelle, my clever kangaroo.
Come to me in the grass in the animal night,
far from people and thinking, just me and wild you,
far from rooms, beyond rules, beyond tamed appetite.

Greta Bolger

JET BOAT STYLE

You are taking swimming lessons
at the Sterling Center YMCA.
I pitch forward on the
aluminum bleacher to witness
the semi-finals of scoop paddle,
the nationals of floating.

Your shoulder straps ride side saddle
and your hair sasses me back already.
Still, now, it is impossible for you
to be an A & P queen, a bathing suit girl
because you are five.

Mrs. Seal hands out noodles and
clicks your hunchback bubble.
You carbonate that water while she barks out metaphors:
"Butterfly arms," "Cannonball," "Legs like scissors."
You tell me "My hair is jet boat style, Mama."
"Thick as waves."
And I know you don't need our language,
working your own words.

Sometimes you scrawl comment cards
at the Sterling Center YMCA
because you know what you need.
You growl your desires – more bubbles
longer shower, corn muffins at snack bar-
like an inmate with a list of demands if you
are to endure your small container.

In the locker room, the manatees from the ten o'clock
water aerobics crackle complaints of cold water,
dusting their underpants with powder,
standing on non-skid soles.
But a five year old can't get cold
a motor-boat, motor-boat circulates just under the skin.

After class, you defy that timed shower,
hitting the button again to fill your small suit.
You work to trap the water between fabric and skin,
teaching your body to puff out proud,
making a temporary new form and
learning the lesson of water's sensation.

Colleen Michaels

Ira Joel Haber

LEARNING TO DRAW

It took one of your pictures
for me to get the concept
of shape. Round circles
so that you pass through
the constriction of fear
like a beam of light
traveling through a tube
capturing enough
dedicated energy
so that darkness
is itself the one threatened.

Straight lines
to teach you about deception
that all things linear
will eventually
fold back against themselves,
that it might be best
to admit to imperfections
avoid the suffocation
of never finding
another shape.

You give me trees.
Flowers. Winged fairies
with their almond eyes
and triangular mouths
who live on jagged mountains
surrounded by light
unafraid to look up
and catch snowflakes
on their tongues
each with their own
unique pattern.

Angela S. Hooper

LESSON LEARNED

It's the same every Saturday. As we pull into the school parking lot my son stops talking. And smiling. He gets a look on his face that's rarely there, yet not unfamiliar. A look of resignation coupled with determination. Not unlike the look of an animal that knows its been cornered by a predator, but chooses to fight anyway.

As we walk down the empty hallway, he takes my hand - something he rarely does anymore. Before I open the door he looks up and asks, "You'll stay the whole time, won't you?" I nod. We go in. Another morning of basketball.

Inside the gym it is moistly warm, and smells of too many bodies. The noise generated by two dozen seven-year-olds running, dribbling balls and shouting bounces off the walls and floor creating an incoherent cacophony of sound. I find a corner to claim as my own away from the other parents.

Conor walks slowly to the box where balls are kept. None are left and he turns to me with a look of panic. I pantomime him joining one of the other boys. He moves to the center of the court and simply stands there, as if hoping a ball will magically land in his arms. No boy complains if another grabs a rebound or steals a ball, but no one will simply pass a ball to those who are empty handed. Each must create their own opportunities.

Conor waits and watches, his eyes red rimmed. It is as if he has a small electric fence around him, arms dangling at his sides, shoulders slightly hunched.

Whistles blow. The coaches gather the boys to run drills, practice shots and offer pointers.

Conor listens. And watches. He listens, even as some of the other boys goof off, tickling each other, making funny faces and generally not listening. The intensity of his concentration brings a flush to his face. He watches as each boy steps up and takes a shot. Some swagger, barely taking a look before shooting. Others bounce it two, five, ten times before lofting it into the air. Not all sink it every time, but all have made a basket.

When it's his turn, he carefully places his feet on the line, cradles the ball, eyes the basket, dribbles once. Then throws the ball up. I hold my breath.

The ball passes futilely beneath the basket, not even touching the backboard. Head down, Conor turns and trudges to the end of the line, glancing briefly at me. I smile slightly. God, I wish. I wish just once the ball would leave his hands and sail blithely through the basket with just a hint of a swish.

And therein is the struggle. As I watch, I want to tell him he doesn't have to do this. I want to assure him he's wonderful at so many other things — a wiz at making people laugh, puzzling out computer programs, creating YouTube worthy home videos; even, unfortunately, at burping quite loudly on command.

But I don't. Because if I do, then I'm acknowledging to him — and myself — that he can't play basketball, that perhaps he isn't an athlete. Though who cares? I shouldn't. I don't.

The hour ends. The crowd of now sweaty boys and dads do a group high-five, then peel off to gather balls and jackets. Conor comes over. I offer a few words of encouragement. Already, he's standing straighter, and his eyes no longer have a hunted look. As we walk back down the empty hallway and breathe the fresh air in the parking lot, he begins talking.

"Mom, did you know Mt. Everest is the tallest mountain in the world? And you need an oxygen tank to breathe on top? Do you know what country it's in? Cuz I do. It's two countries — Nepal and Tibet. Cool, huh? Hey, can Joey come over to play?"

Listening to him, I experience an epiphany. My kid can't do everything. Struggling to learn new things is part of is part of growing up, and if we just let our kids have a bit of struggle, they'll be OK. They already know that life isn't easy, nor is it fair — nor can they be the best at everything. It's the adults who have forgotten that lesson.

Julie Cline

I KILL EVERY STUFF

"I kill the door," he says, pointing
his broken windshield wiper.
"I kill the table. I kill every stuff."

He makes prison bars
out of masking tape, and
escapes them. He turns
a paper towel into
a car tunnel.

The point is he can make every stuff,
so whatever he kills, don't worry,
he'll replace it.

Jessy Randall

SUGARY FLUFF

Because you are a good boy
and I want your world
to be filled with only the best,
I fed you a cake with coconut icing
dyed cartoon-ocean blue,
rimmed by gummy octopi
with tentacles twined in friendship,
and topped with Swedish fish kissing,
blowing M&M bubbles into hearts.

Later, when you brought it all up again,
I noted which pieces were hardest to digest
(and these were the same ones
that gave me trouble too)
and vowed to remember that you,
even in wanting to please me,
are just as intolerant as I
of sugary fluff.

Amanda Skjeveland

how i learned to let go (in honor of father's day)

Saturday, June 20, 2009 at 8:04pm

since my son was little, i have always been particular about his environment. except for a three-month hiatus, he has only attended african or muslim schools. he was in karate at three, drumming at four, and manhood training at seven (and still continues them all). and of course there's the football. (booo!) over the years, i've been to more awards ceremonies, school assemblies, championship games and end of year productions than i can count. at all of them i clapped, hollered (to his embarrassment and secret pride) and took pictures when i could. sometimes his grandmother, great-grandmother, or cousins would come, and he was so much the happier. but this year something different happened— his father came.

i have a mostly accurate reputation as a person that is too hard-headed for my own good. or, like my pops says, i gotta get beat up, battered and bruised before i can sit down to learn. but, i believe the universe loves me, and guides people and circumstances into my life to teach me lessons i'm supposed to learn. this lesson came in the form of a good sista-friend, who turns her children over to their father every weekend and just about any other time he wants them. this father doesn't work regularly. he's a hustler—he can build things, tear them apart, move you in or out of a space, and has a van for hire. he lives in his mother's house. and he loves his children. i have seen him bring them his own home cooked meals, and show up all hours of the day and night to pick them up or drop them off wherever they have to go. sometimes, my friend tells me that a month or two has gone by, and he hasn't put anything in her hand. but every friday night, he comes for his children. "their father has something to give them," she says. "it might not always be money. it might be a day at the park, or a story, or a hot meal- but he has something for them, and they have a right to it."

now. my son has been in schools and activities since he was three years old, and his father never asked me how much anything cost, or if we needed a ride to or from anywhere. (he drives, i don't.) we once went half & half on school tuition for four months and then he disappeared around new year's and i had to take my son out of school. my son and i have traveled on buses, trains and in cabs, one or both of us sick or well, in all boroughs, in all kinds of weather, at any time of day or night. so of course i'm upset when his father shows up to take him out for pizza.

pizza? pay some school fees. he needs shoes, not chuck e. cheese.
but my friend broke it down to me. she said, "if the only memory your son ever has of his father is eating pizza, why would you take that away from him? when he gets to be a man, he's gonna be glad he got a meal with his father. he's always up under women, you, your mother, your grandmother. let him be up under some men. his father got something for him." (this friend likes to make long speeches. that's just an excerpt from a much longer sermon.)

eventually, she was the one who convinced me to start letting my son go out into the world with his father. and whenever his father did something irresponsible, like picking him up or dropping him off hours late, or bringing him back so stuffed with junk food that he vomited the minute he stepped into the door, i would call my friend up in rage or frustration and she would sigh and laugh a little and say, "thank god, he has a father. isn't it wonderful?" (insert @#$%!!!&*! here)

in time, i came to see the truth. and the truth is a funny thing. sometimes it doesn't look anything like we want it to look. because here i was criss-crossing the city and going into debt to make sure my son had all these activities, and yet i could see his little back straighten with a word from his father. and my son had a new place carved out for himself when the other kids got together on the playground or at school, shouting, "my father said.." and the new place was that he no longer had to be an observer. he could jump in and say, "my father..." too. and i saw that he was proud, and i didn't want to be the one to take that pride away.

so here we are at the present day. he is ten and for the first time last week, he had both parents at his performance. his father's other sons, his little brothers, were there. my mother was there. we all sat together and talked about the children in the show. we cheered for my son when he came onstage and his brothers called his name. his father, this man who, i believe, has never had someone give him private school,
or karate, or drumming, and who had to find his way on the streets of brooklyn without manhood training, was full of love for his son. i saw his shoulders push back as he sat up taller and hushed the younger children, saying, "look, your brother." I saw the joy on his face that his seed was good. never mind the arguments between us, the constant lack of money, the small things about who picked up and who dropped off and when. somehow, between us both, and the families that come with us, the child has been given what he needs, and the seed is good.

after the show, my son's chest was puffed out so wide i wondered how he didn't tip over. his father didn't say anything much to him, and at one time i would have criticized that. i would have thought, he didn't even congratulate the child. his father just laid a hand on his shoulder and it was fine. and when my son and his brothers raced up and down the theater steps, tumbling a little too wild in the night air, i stepped forward, but their father was watching and i let it be. and when his father gave me something in my hand, and it was less than i expected, i wanted to ask him what he thought such a small amount could do. but probably, in two weeks or so, there would be a little more. so i gave thanks. sometimes, when i wanna boil me up a plate of hot grits and sit in the doorway waiting on him, i just remind myself to breathe. my son is almost a teenager now and soon what's between those two will be man business. and my son has a father. (isn't it wonderful?)

Radhiyah Ayobami

WHAT THE PHOTO SHOWS

I savor what the photo shows from that day
when winter mist cradled us between the marshy
toes of Annapurna and Ganesh Himal,
how it helps us remember
where red bougainvillea, red powdered rice, and tangerines spilled
over green leaf plates held together by twigs,
where a green papaya anchored smoking incense sticks,
where a pole swaddled in greenery pillared one corner of the canopy,
how handsome you looked in a *kurta salwar* and *Dhaka topi*,
how well you bowed your forehead,
how Youngest Uncle, warmed by a red sweater, tilted his feet up to
  meet your forehead,
how he looked at the camera,
and smiled

But we both know what the photo doesn't show,
like the *pukka* blessing just a few minutes before,
when you really and truly became
one with the Vedas,

one with your father's ancestors
and your future progeny,
one with Shiva, Vishnu, Prithvi,
when you became a man —
and except for the stain from my foreign womb —
almost Brahman,
how men, and women in red, said
stop,
how the priests put down their Vedas
and joined the chant:

A camera.
A camera.
Somebody bring
a camera.

And someone did,
and the priests said, do it again.
So once again you bowed your forehead,
stained by red tika,
to Honorary Guru's feet.
Click. Click. Still not right, still not
right, the priests said.
One more time. Just one
more. And this time,
they said to Youngest Uncle,
look at
the camera.

Elizabeth Enslin

OBJECT PARADE: EGGS

My mother taught me to separate eggs. A clean break against the stainless bowl, and then this high-wire act: the halves cradled in the fingertips of each hand, shifting the yolk back and forth from shell to shell, and letting the white — clear and gooey — drip into the bowl, until nothing left but that quivering yellow heart, which was thrown down the disposal, or slipped to one of the dogs, or saved for a hollandaise and poured over my broccoli at supper. Meanwhile, the whites, whipped to a froth, then to sturdy peaks, then molded and baked in the oven, and that's where the story comes in: how I was just five when I separated the eggs for my own birthday cake (or maybe I only watched and clapped from the counter). A picture somewhere, layers frosted in chocolate and decorated with faux mushrooms, as miraculous as the ones sprung up whole overnight after a rain, but fashioned from meringue — egg whites and sugar — and consequently disappointing. Too sweet and airy for me. Devoted as I was to dense and savory even then, I'd have been just as delighted to blow out my candles in a three-egg omelet.

But don't we forget about eggs? Don't we talk about them as if they're no big deal? Delicate though they are, hasn't their preparation — as default breakfast — become metaphor and evidence of ordinary competence? She can't even boil an egg, we sneer, and the implication is clear. So when my own son, 16 years old, well over six feet tall– he shaves! He drives!-- asks me this morning if I'll boil him a few, break up the toast in the bowl the way he likes, I realize, it's not that he needs me to wait on him; it's only that he truly doesn't know how. I've witnessed his enthusiasm in the kitchen: elaborate feasts involving mountains of eggs — scrambled, or fried — with ham, sausage, salami, varieties of breads and spreads; the accompanying utensils at the ready — whisks, spatulas, wooden spoons, graters — more than one frying pan going at once, even. But the fact of a boiled egg has him stymied. Entertained as I am by his culinary athleticism (I've long since stopped wincing when he breaks an egg into a pan), by the vigor with which he goes after his breakfast, whacking it against the side of the skillet, leaving a trail of sticky white in its wake, shell fragments, too — it never occurred to me to offer instruction. Long ago, in fact, with no thought to finesse, I taught him instead the trick of removing those elusive little chippings. He's an expert now, goes after them with another bigger piece of same — works like a charm (or a magnet) every time.

But — who knew? Who remembered? — to prepare a soft-boiled egg from start to finish is no simple task. To lift it from the water before the yolk begins to cook is only a matter of timing, sure. But to crack it open without getting burned; to scoop it out without losing most of the white to the membrane, the yolk to the counter; to get breakfast to the table before the yellow starts to congeal: it's worth a demonstration, isn't it? I'll teach you, I say.

This morning's lesson then: Three four-minute-eggs with two slices of toasted rye. Watch, I say, after the timer goes off; one purposeful snap of the wrist at the edge of a blue and white china bowl, then I scoop the shells clean with a spoon. Your turn, I say. And this boy — this champion! — is afraid of his egg. He bites his lip, holds his breath, plays for time as if this really were the high trapeze: gingerly, he taps... A glance in my direction. Tap, tap. Nothing. C'mon now, I say, and I hand him the spoon. Try with this. And then a bludgeoning — a murderous act — and removing the edible portion is no less violent. My boy, very sober and with no small amount of deference, hands me the third egg.

 "I'll butter the toast," he says.

Dinah Lenney

PATTERNS

I
In high school sewing class we would-be women
labored over patterns – tracing and pinning paper brittle-thin
as cicada wings. We shared scissors and kissing experience,
made clumsy attempts at zippers, double pleats, French button holes.

II
In a trunk full of boxed-up challenges I find them: patterns
for prom confections, romantic dirndls and peasant shirts;
remnants of impulsive choices, passing enthusiasms intended
for velvet, moiré, and brocade.

III
A self-taught seamstress, my mother fashioned my girlhood
wardrobe from my imagination and her wits. At the mercy
of our budget and my fantasies she cut her own patterns
from newspaper, used gift wrap, and grocery bags.

Late into the night her treadle machine whirred
like a movie reel with a stylish child star. By high school
I chafed at her limitations, made no secret of my longing for store-
bought brands, or how I envied the smart styles others wore.

IV
They dance before me now, her brave attempts at harmony
and haute couture: girlish creations with their fuss and frills dampened
by mutual frustration, but each one finished down to the last bright button,
the hem of each whispery skirt.

Teddy Norris

Self-portrait:

under a yellow crayon sun—

between trees of green scalloping on tall brown trunks—

her daughter: a tiny figure on spiky grass

contextualized, she said, within a greater world

understanding you are not the center

the other girls balloon from the belly of their page.

round cheeks press the rectangle, splurge off the edge

triangle skirts let their corners drip

my mother found them fat, entitled

the sun does not figure here

neither do the trees

Ana C. H. Silva

Ira Joel Haber

CONVERSATION '66

"Am I beautiful?" I ask my mother. We're standing at the kitchen counter near the spot where her Mixmaster sits.

"You are very pretty," she says. "But study hard. Be a nurse and marry a doctor. It's as easy to marry a rich man as a poor one. There are so many books I loved as a girl. Now put the dough onto the cookie sheets like this. Scoop with one spoon, scrape with the other."

"Like this?"

"Now make the salad like this. I'll make the meat and the vegetables and the potatoes. You cut out the biscuits like this. And the water for the piecrust has to be cold. Use an ice cube—like this. You know you can drown in a cup of water. Drink eight glasses a day. Wait an hour after eating before swimming. And never ever swim alone.

But choose your friends wisely. Birds of a feather flock together. A bird in the hand is worth two in the bush. Beggars can't be choosers. And remember you cannot have your cake and eat it, too.

Now set the table with the knife blade turned toward the plate like this. The spoon goes next to it. The fork goes on the left—like this. Drink all your milk. Eat your meat. That Twiggy is too damn thin and there are children starving in China.

You iron your father's handkerchiefs like this. I'll do his shirts. Pin the pattern to the fabric like this. Press your knee against the sewing machine lever like this. You make the apron, I'll make the dress.

Knit one, purl two. Yarn over, yarn over, like this.

Now blot your lipstick like this. Brush your hair one hundred strokes each night before bed like this. A woman's hair is her crowning glory. Wash your face with cold water so it shrinks the pores. Splash it ten times like this.

Hook it and turn it. Shake yourself in like this. Stand up straight. Practice good posture by walking with a book on your head. That's how models do it.

This is a booklet about the things you need to know. Here's where I keep the Kotex. It goes on like this. Soak the blood out in cold water.

Blood is thicker than water. Like this.
Don't look me in the eye and lie to me. If you tell one lie, you'll have to tell two. If you tell two lies, you'll have to tell three."

"But am I beautiful?" I ask my mother.

"Speak up," she says. "The squeaky wheel gets the grease."

Denise Emanuel Clemen

Ellen Rix

CBT

Have you heard from Aunt Millie yet? What's her advice to you on home training?

RHD

What did she say to you about bringing up the girls?

CBT

Listen to what she said to me...

When yuh wake up in de morning clean de yampee out yuh eyes.
Say morning to de neighbor only if she watch yuh and yuh eye make four
If not, mind yuh business.
Remember yuh mother home training, yuh father eh ha no home training
So what I say GOES

RHD

*Don't look big people in the eyes like you ah big woman
Remember, girl chile bound to bring you grief, once she menses COME
is man she drawing like flies
Being born a girl is a curse. You hear me. A curse.*

CBT

Your name is GIRL, keep yuh elbow off de table, don't talk with food in yuh mouth
wash yuh stink salfish before supper and twice when yuh have de visitor
soak de dirty menstral diaper in cold water for 3 hours,
soak it again, then
Scrub it on de jukking board, then lay it in de sun so de stain could bleach out

RHD
*You have you monthlies
Stop pitching marbles
Pelting mango
Climbing trees
Talking to boys
Except is child you want*

Lesson 3   Make sure the church bell ring. Just don't bring no nappy headed child here.

CBT

Love? Where yuh pick up them scraps of love
by the roadside?
Make sure the church bell ring first
before yuh open up yuh legs, yuh hear me.
Girl, ugly like you so, have to take what you get.
Sometimes you have to buy cat in bag.
And, remember, if you make baby, without de wedding ring
I making nine nights for you, like dey do for the dead.
Because to me, you dead.

RHD

You better be glad some man want you for wife
is not everyday girl like you does get lucky so.
so what if he violent when he drink he rum.....
Huh....
Don't play stupid here for me, nuh
If it wasn't something you doing   something you showing
you wouldn't get you ass in this bacchanal
you don't have nobody to blame but yourself.
You can't call that rape when you dress like that.

Lesson 4   You better get a damn job. Smile to hide your ugly shame.

CBT

Poet!?
What poet? That is job too.
Poetry does make money?
Who go buy dem pretty words?
Success....if you call that success
look here gurl
keep yuh elbow off de table
don't talk with food in yuh mouth
don't sing at de table
and smile, girl ugly as you must always smile
And, for sure you better get a damn job.
Poet! What poet!

RHD

What you mean, you want to fire the work.
If the Syrian man in the fabric shop
want to touch you up down dey,
you just let him. No harm in that.
What you mean….the meager salary he paying you
don't cover that. What stupidness you talking, girl.
You better be glad somebody hire you with that picky head.
Take you little black ass and go do the man work, you hear me.

Lesson 5   Wash up three times to cut the blight of being born girl.

CBT

Yuh don't know is evening.   Yuh name is girl child.
Wash twice, three times if you have to.
Yuh smell like a horse. Yuh thin, thin, thin, like ah fish line,
one eye brown, the other…I not sure….one set ah gold teeth
in front yuh mouth. Yuh so should wash three times, if yuh plan to get ah man,
Unless yuh making Zami and is rub up you want to rub up on woman.

RHD

Go down by the bay
take this calabash
and three green limes
cut in half.
Stoop down at the edge of the ocean
dip the calabash in the water
squeeze the green limes
rub juice all over yuh body
even down dey, between yuh legs
dip sea water and throw over your head
three times. Stand up. Walk backwards
to cut the blight, because yuh name is girl.

Lesson 6, 7, 8, 9, & 10   Be happy.   Your name is girl.

Wash good. Scrape the lust from yuh hands

Whose hands hold the rosary beads

Laugh stale. Cling to your thin hair.

Hail Mary, Mother of God. Five times.

Hold on tight, cuddle your defiant belly

Pray. You better pray.

Kiss the lovable rage.

Pray. You better pray.

Live wide in the world.

Lie still. Camouflage. Be Girl.

Cheryl Boyce-Taylor & RH Douglas

THE FAMILY LINE

My father liked his wine enough
to keep a gallon in the bedroom closet
for after dinner, over the quota

my mother allowed, in the basement
another gallon along with scotch.
My grandfather kept the jug

next to his chair. Children got a splash
in their Seven-Up to make it pink.
Great-grandfathers drank at the head

of the table. The women washed dishes,
cooked and washed more dishes.
My mother had one scotch only

on special occasions, giggled,
said she was tipsy, excuse to call
my father a fuck and bastard

as he went   down   down   down
through the years.
Those women needed drugs,

medicinal not recreational, life skills,
self-awareness, an examination
of conscience, an impact study,

instead of making cabled sweaters
and embroidered tablecloths,
stuffed artichokes and arancini,

while the men counted their money,
cleaned guns, collected stamps
and women. They drank wine,

taught the line to say everything
was fine, fine, fine, left me a legacy
I'm still swallowing.

Joan Mazza

PATTERN

Giving and giving as women
were taught by generations
of mothers. Giving out of
nothing. That is something
only the goddess can expect
to continue forever.

Once we denied our daughters
to feed our sons, as if
their importance was inherent.

Now our work is with girls.
And women, wherever they are.
learning and teaching and learning
more.

Penn Kemp

Ellen Rix

SWEET WILLIAM FOR A DAUGHTER-IN-LAW

Poem for Deisha

My son brings home the daughter I have longed for, she is Sweet William
and Rubrium lilies, delicate and strong   she's smaller than I expect,
since I know he is a tit man
small in stature, large in character
Yeolin, my former mother-in-law, has taught me the hardest lesson of all

                    how to crush a young
                    daughter-in-law

I have promised myself and the universe… no matter what girl my son
brings home, I will love her like my own daughter.

                    I will keep my word.

That thanksgiving he brings her home
after dinner he makes each of us tell him why she should be his bride
she laughs heartily not at all bothered by his showmanship.
                    I can tell she is ready for a show biz man

               later she fixes my hair with the flat iron
               tells me she did this with her mother
                    how she misses her now that she has gone

my heart makes a lei around hers
she's mine

Cheryl Boyce-Taylor

INCARNATION

Robyn Beattie

You've chosen this house,
some say, or inherited it:

when finished looking in, look out
through the eyes of your children,

or try. Be gentle with yourself;
trapped in each wound, healers say,

is the salve to heal it: poison oak
on a forest floor: walk, look,

within ten feet: its antidote,
the soap plant. Descend, hidden

blue-print stuck to your spinal cord
at birth, like the tail pinned on the donkey,

except you can't hand it off to the next
child in line. If it's a game, spinning

with a blindfold isn't fun—
inner ear confusing north with south,

up with down, and you're left dizzy,
listening for the sound of your mother's voice

steering you away from the jeering curve
of the rest of the party. Learn

who to trust, who to ignore. Soon
you must find your way on your own.

Tania Pryputniewicz

FOR NOTICING

I suppose you've noticed Mother
That I no longer want you
To tuck me in at night.
I am too old to be
Tempted by breath.
Or the rush of kiss,
A runaway rescued. Or my
Sheets smoothed as a shield.
I suppose you've noticed
I am your big girl now.

Catherine Woodard

Robyn Beattie

CELIE AT FOUR

The way you say
"I know THAT,"
impatient,
wanting to get on
to the next thing.
You mean
you now know it
because I just told you.
You're too fast for me,
at four, you're
seventeen and I'm
the little sister
wanting to be liked.

Jessy Randall

RING OF FIRE

"But love doesn't burn," she said,
and I didn't tell her—*Yes it does,
little girl. It burns,
burns, burns,
even this: mother
to daughter, daughter to mother*—
just turned up the radio,
raised my voice.

Amy Watkins

WHAT THE BODY CARRIES

Delicious tushy. That's what you had.
I couldn't get enough. Your thighs too –
a fistful of *pulkies*, chubby chicken legs.

Your tush is now a butt, delicious still
but I don't say a word, don't even
call you *baby*. This is the right thing,
I suppose, not to squeeze my girl's

behind. I wonder if your body
        remembers all that focus and fuss
                at the plump rise under a blanket,
                        or the bounce in a run from the bath. Gone,

my complete possession.
        Hands in lap, unsettled,
                I learn new words, give you *space*,
                        Chill – watch you move down the street,

petrified that anyone will touch you there.
        So covered these days, so shut-door.
                Will you open when ready, call back
                        the glee at your yummiest spots?
                                Keep close to your skin the early cherish,
                                        make it happen again.

Janlori Goldman

Ellen Rix

58

WHAT SHE GAVE HERSELF

I worried when I touched myself
                                                    there,
I might become pregnant,
   my belly filling with something
         other
than ice cream and cake,
   a little something   a handful
of years younger than me –
                                                    there
under the card table, a blanket
   draped over it, deep in my sleeping
            bag, my dad

sunk in his chair, mom
   on the couch, unaware, the TV's blaze
a light to steer by.

                           Years later
I still feel the sweep of an elbow,
   tiny hand, a foot   inside
         the taut
bubble of my stomach.
                     Rare mornings
   I see the sun
                           break water
at lake's edge,
   wishing I could be
                                                    there
at it's birth, my hands bloody,
   midwife
         to all that brilliance.

Ronda Broatch

FIRST BLOOD

(May 7, 2002)

"Your daughter's started her period!"
"What should I do?"
"Nothing, you're the dad.
Dads aren't supposed to know."

10 + 1/2 years is too soon.
She'll figure it all out.
Get it on with tampons, maxi pads, and Advil.
Doesn't seem fair. Showing up so early
when she still wants to be a boy.
Runs faster than any boy.

Of course I don't know about it.
Not invited into the Women Only Blood Club.
Staying clueless - the elegantly simpler gender.

My mind works on an impromptu ole'dad-soft-shoe
        circle of women, full moon,
        the ebb and the flow,
        women's secrets, sisterhood,
        and the Goddess Girl's Club,
but it's not working. Nothing sacred about any of this
for me.

When I get home I hug her
"lets go for a coke and a hamburger"
        ...as if nothing's happened.
Just your same old dad. The old safe shoe.
Feeling sad for she who must now bleed in secret,
alone.

Charles Ries

INDIGO SKY IN PORT-AU-PRINCE

I.
With Mother gone to bed, I can sneak out the window, into Ben's car, crushing cigarette butts and torn ticket stubs. My weekend smile squiggles, slinks onto my face as the Chevy blazes down the road, Bob Marley and the Wailers on the eight-track. Ah, the outlaw joy of escape! I'm crossing out of the definite borders of Mother's realm of power. When the tires crunch on the coquina driveway of Cafe Creole, dust dances in a lazy tornado, a flannel blanket around the car.

II.
Dirty neon lights dangle from the ceiling beams; they flicker on and off without rhythm, their wriggly green wires crooked like chicken bones strung together on a string. I hear the music in my chest, vibrating, waiting, a wave that flattens my thoughts, washes them away with a mindless, insistent staccato. I become part of its pulse as it pulls me out of myself with a heightened sense of abandon, unreality.

III.
A tiny slice of yellow, a twisted lemon peel, lies at the bottom of the blue moon in Port-au-Prince's indigo sky. And there's this one fiery star -- blazing. Mother wouldn't let me be Ben's star. "No, you're not going to that night club. For chrissake, you're only fourteen. And I don't like that Ben kid." I rest my cheek on the starched whiteness of Ben's shirt.

IV.
On the dance floor, unhooked pelvises work so butts pivot around their axes. There are cocktail stirrers everywhere, like an abandoned game of pick-up-sticks. Ben is mad because some guy gets me a Prestige beer at the bar. I hear the purr of his engine cranking. Clunk: Ben shifts into gear. I listen as the night gobbles up the humming of his motor. As he disappears. Leaving me in the parking lot of the club, things biting my legs, crawling all over me.

V.
An engine idles beside me. Headlights glare past me now, staring into the path of trodden grass Ben has paved. "Get in," Mother says. She slowly turns the Isuzu Trooper around, pushes play, and doesn't say another word. Bob Marley and the Wailers. The tires spin on the dry gravel. I adjust the rear view mirror: a lazy tornado spins in the distance.

M.J. Fievre

FIRSTS

Howard
mixed rum and coke for me
at Dad's office party.
Last summer we played football,
fought the pine cone wars,
but now we drink
and kiss.

Toothpaste
to take away the taste
of oysters, rum, and tongue.
Sandra and I play xerox games,
then ink our ankles with fake tattoos.
Dad sees me dizzy and laughing
with toothpaste
in my hair.

"Sorry," I say,
and I'm grounded, still
he lets me roll down the window
and hand-surf in the wind despite
his rule about moving vehicles
and limbs that must stay
inside.

Marguerite Scott

TIME TO GO

***

I was born to hike miles with a child on my back and another on the way. Front and back at the same time, and all of us moving forward. I was born to celebrate the construction of structures whose finished heights made small children swoon. I was born to read aloud; the summer we spent with Life of Pi remains an island of serenity in the deeply unpredictable ocean of adolescence. I was born to keep children warm, and so it was with every millimeter of the yarn that slid through my crocheting fingers into the afghan that accompanied my daughter to college. And the quilt, constructed from years of treasured, outgrown blue jeans, that accompanied my second-born. What nature of blanket will warm the heart of my youngest? I will know soon enough.

I was born to be not PTA president, but her neighbor. It isn't local election campaigns that have me racing home from work, but a hunger for my kids. When my firstborn explodes in cascades of confusion, I whirl and blurt out, "I've never been mother to a 14-year-old girl before. They didn't give me a practice set!" My children teach me what I didn't know in that lusterless time before.

I was born to cultivate individuality, but I have not yet realized that this is a march toward obsolescence. So when she cuts the cord, I am convinced that it is my daughter, and not I, who has come undone. Her cancelled cell phone "a waste of resources," I call her land line. She is indignant.

My husband is fascinated by the gale-force strength of my despair. I try to be philosophical instead of inconsolable. Maybe she's a chrysalis, metamorphosing from fuzzy caterpillar into graceful butterfly. Or a bird. I once choreographed my daughter's departure. Her wings strong and shiny, she would step onto the ledge, right foot first. Her downward-facing palm would alight on my outstretched hand with just enough contact to maintain her erect posture. Then she would fly away, like the robin whose maiden voyage I witnessed as it flew from the nest above our porch.

Instead, she looks, hops, and drops to the ground, where friends gather by pre-arranged signal to catch her. Down below, I see my daughter brushing herself off. It's an in-between stage, I try to reassure myself -- as if anything isn't. I hug her long-abandoned, stuffed teddy.

***

Just before my young husband and I depart for a year overseas, my new mother-in-law asks us to call once a month. "To check in," she says. My husband inhales, looks at me, and slowly says, "We'll write." Later that year, after Anwar Sadat, president of Egypt, is assassinated, my husband calls. Half-joking, his mother says, "If it's not safe for Sadat, it's not safe for you." "I'll take that under advisement," says my smiling husband. "That means go to hell," she responds brightly. We stay, return home for 6 months, and leave again, unapologetic, for a second year.

Another time, I spend spring break in my dorm with a cute guy and a hot plate. My sister calls to report that our mother is in tears. Her words seem beside the point; my plans have nothing to do with my mother. I never acknowledge them in any way. Until now.

***

My mother visits her granddaughter, and gives her insights into her newly minted independence. I call to check in. Mom reports that our offspring is an original. "She has her own way of doing things." "Like her mother," she adds, pausing, "and her grandmother." I feel a small wisp of relief.

Some thirty years ago, my journeys enriched my life beyond measure. In planes and dreams, I returned to the places I first visited as a young woman, but I never thought what more I was passing on. I would like to bow out gracefully, but I cannot. My daughter will have to wrest this one from me. I am still learning to live with the choices I made.

Roxanne B Sukol

PROVIDENCE

A girl asks the universe for praise.
Instead, it gives her rain which fills her
small row boat. She is alone at sea,
as she has been for many days.
Her mind is stormy. She can't think
to bail. While she curses clouds,
the vessel sinks. Inside the collar of a life
vest she finds written in black
where a sailor's name should be
the word "beautiful."
She puts it on.

Carolee Sherwood

Kim McMecham

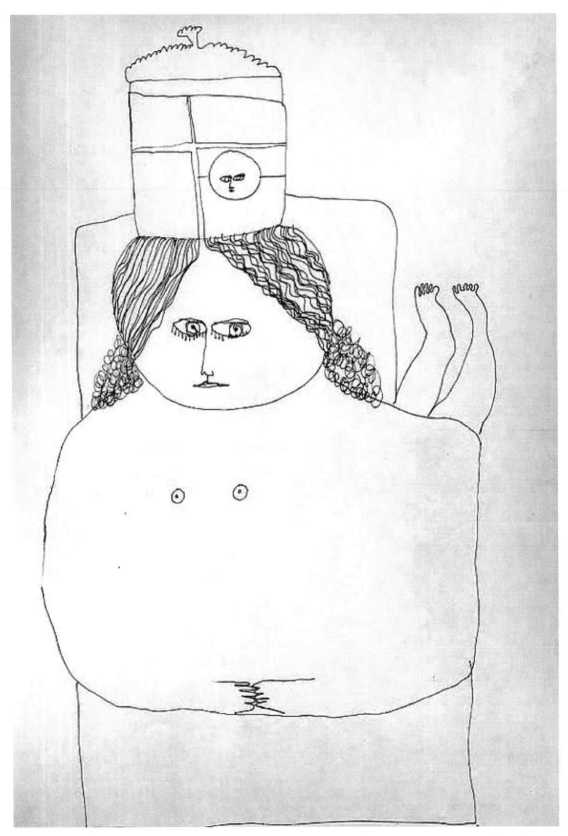

Ira Joel Haber

A BAG OF HAMMERS

When I ask my girlfriends,
what guidance did your grandmothers give?,
What powerful warnings, helpful hints
did they offer as you made your way?

Maria says, my grandmother used to tell us:
Always follow a donkey.
It will lead you to a village
by nightfall.

But, never follow a goat.
It will take you to the edge
of a cliff.

Jamika repeats what her mothers recited:
You wanna be a nobody, do nothing.

My own mother constantly voiced:
Trouble comes in a thousand shapes.

And her Irish mother, Philomena, who died young
believed: *Life is short, and so we must*
go through it slowly.

But Valerie's grandmother possessed the most
insightful similes about her boyfriends.
Dumb as dirt, she would say.
He's as dumb as a bag of hammers.
He's so dumb
 he couldn't pour water out of a boot
if the directions were on the heel.

As Valerie drove off with her latest love,
her grandmother would shake her head sadly:
A lost ball in the high weeds.

Gail Ghai

JAR

Knuckles, wrists, clenched white
as lice writhing

by candlelight one humid night
with a lover hung like Mapplethorpe

before our move and my affair
with middle ground—

not making do, but the extremes:
sea flooding soil rootless

from overuse, long rows
of full-grown corn shaking

like storm-wracked birds
at water's edge. Switchbacks

to counteract the vertigo
of inbetween—

La Passionata laughed my dad,
your mother's dominant red gene.

I, too, married a scientist; potential
of reactive molecules, excess light

energy. A jar of water shattered
on the wall. Paintings proffered

in haste against apologies.

Kirstin Hotelling Zona

WHEN I WOKE UP AND SAW YOUR BIKE GONE

(for Pablo, the almost step-son)

When I woke up and saw your bike gone,
I found the hole in my heart.

Wasn't it locked up?
I felt the wind on my face.

And followed you
Across the Brooklyn Bridge,

Arms outstretched. You were in the lead.
Your father behind us.

Hadn't I crossed this bridge before, you said?
I thought of Pablo Neruda,

"How can anyone tire of such magnificence?"

I watched you skateboard across the planks.
You noticed some were dark and others light.

I thought to myself, the boy is scientific!
Stay brilliant as each new day's sun.

And when the weather is less than fine,
Find the love to say it.

Kathryn M. Fazio

RESISITANCE

(Excerpt from In Search of Paprika: Reflections on an Intercultural Marriage)

We were married in the one thousandth, nine hundredth and eighty-ninth year of the Christian calendar. Even though we married before a Justice of the Peace without any regard for a white dress, I considered our marriage a celestial miracle. Our orbiting masses were pulled to fusion by divine magnetic force. Our marriage would become an oversized billboard for the future's multiculturalism. His Pakistani, Muslim family however, privately doomed the union to cataclysmic combustion. Mine held their breaths while swearing support of my most *grown-up* decision.

It never occurred to his parents that he would marry a *firenghi* even though they had lived in this country since he was twelve. He was such a *good boy*, combed, obedient and successful, and there had been no warning. No girlfriends. No drinking nor disrespect. So they were shocked when their eldest son told them of his intentions.

"Please. Don't do it, *Behta*," his *Abbu* cajoled affectionately. "It will not work. They do not have our ways." When logic failed, he sat numb at the fringes of female hysteria.

"Ayyyyy. What of my boy's happiness?" his *Amma* wept inconsolably. So spastic were her intakes of air and snot, that there was almost a primal quality to her distress. "What will they say about us in the community?" she wailed.

But she knew. How the aunties would commiserate and wag their heads. *Aiiii il laaaaa. They tried soooo many times to introduce him to girls – ve-ry bhew-ti-ful girls. Fair and charming. And from such good fam-i-lies.*

Lingering, we lived at the edges of his family's upheaval. Having watched just a few of their Bollywood movies, I recognized our drama's script: the tragic yearning of resisted lovers; a mother's heartbreak morphing into life-threatening ailments; the painful unraveling of a knitted family. Yet, we had tampered with the familiar plot. My Salaams were those of an Amrikan and my Blackness felt twisted and swollen in a story line it didn't belong.

"Why don't you stand up to them?" I challenged. After all, it had been seven years. "If you tell them what you're going to do, all this will stop. They'll accept us as a couple. We'll be happy; I know it." I considered their outlandish cackle, their immigrant fears for their son and our dreams, mawkish masks for true devotion.

"Just give me more time. It will destroy them if I go through with this right now."

"But what about me?" I pleaded.

Now, my parents love as parents should, I'd thought to myself. In a synchronized dance that my mother and I knew by heart, she only questioned me, hoping my lead and her shadowy suggestions might prompt me to consider something more. "What about the children? And Christmas?" Wary, she'd still smiled.

But my parents had modeled a strong, independent woman from their shared histories of struggle. It took your great, great grandfather they'd said, mulatto son of a slave owner, to buck the law and bequeath land to his Negroid descendants. It had demanded my grandfather, a strapping, Baptist minister in Mississippi, look down a rifle barrel rather than back down a bridge to allow a white man to pass first. And, it had taken both my parents to leave the suburbs and enroll themselves at Harvard, just to make a difference. Family had sculpted me and they were proud of a job, well done.

But perhaps it is difficult to calibrate devotion by the nature of our parents' protests. For who is to say whether acceptance or resistance defines the greater love? Now a parent, I know how resolute is a mother's love for the hollow, bony pocket behind a scraped knee. And I know how crippling to a child's flight, is a parent's crush of love.

My husband and I would persevere, determined to marry. Moral conviction and intellectual certitude propelled me to fight although I understand now that I was but one of many masses hurtling through the stratosphere, and that our two celestial bodies colliding may have been more random than anything else. My fervor intoxicated my husband with power he had never known. Yet twenty years into our marriage, I realize our battle was not about me. Perhaps our mothers, in the pits of their stomachs, knew our most grown-up decision would commit us to a marriage of much harder work than most. A marathon where I can only hope breathing deeply and pacing myself allows us to finish the course.

Lisa Argrette Ahmad

FALL: A LESSON

Long before my divorce (final by age 24, "no fault" according to the papers), Alan said I appeared corn-fed as he sipped a martini in Eve's backyard. Filled with flowers, wild and full, that yard looked nothing like the carefully mowed squares behind houses in Lakeland. Branches from giant old trees hung low, resting on the roof and brushing on the windows. My father would have trimmed those branches years back, would have never allowed those trees to get so out of hand.

Alan wore a white button-up shirt, un-tucked and un-ironed, with dark blue jeans and leather flip-flop sandals. Wore the same thing every day to work at the small gallery he directed, the gallery where I just started to work. He shaved his head, avoiding the appearance of a 50-something man with gray and thinning hair. He spoke with what I imagined to be a New York accent – gruff and quick -- and smelled of clove cigarettes. He drank quickly and with a smile.

I sipped my first martini. Strong. Tasted like pine sap. I tried not to flinch. New England roasted on that hot August evening. My hair (still down to my shoulders, sides pulled back tight in a simple barrette, front bangs curled under) frizzed. I held a chunk of my light cotton skirt in my free hand and swayed it through the air to create a breeze, something completely unnecessary back home where the wind blew constant.

I mulled the meaning of his assessment but had no response. I used to eat corn, lots of it, this time of year when farmers hauled loads of fresh-picked sweet corn in the back of their trucks, parking at the busy intersection in town to sell it -- $3 for a dozen ears plus one. Mom boiled it on the stove and then coated each ear with butter and salt. But I knew he didn't mean sweet corn. Corn-fed like cattle? Didn't that cause all those diseases? Or corn-fed like pigs? While not exactly thin (my husband often mocked my thick thighs) I appeared sturdy, but not fat. Was corn out of vogue among New England artists? Or did corn just mean Iowa?

I took another drink of the pine sap -- a longer one this time. It went down smoother than the first. I dug out one of the blue-cheese stuffed olives resting at the bottom of the glass. It tasted salty, bitter, interesting. I scooped up another, and then washed it down.
You're a good kid, he said, but a little young to be married, right?
I stood before him, 22 years of age, and entirely convinced that

my age not only qualified me to be a wife but necessitated it. That day marked my six week anniversary. I'd been in New England for five of those weeks, following a honeymoon to the Wisconsin Dells. I shrugged.

So what do you think of it out here?

I took another long drink. Oh, I love it, I said honestly and – because I could not have answered any other way at that moment in time -- without pretension. It's so beautiful! The hills, the old churches and graveyards and houses! And the town squares, and the historical sites, and all the colleges, of course the trees! It's so different from home with the winding roads and green hills! In Lakeland ...

He smiled and interrupted, uninterested in the rest of my response. Wait till fall he said with a wink. He patted my floral print-covered ass as he walked toward the small bar on Eve's patio.

I finished my drink in one big swig. I savored the tingle running through my veins as the martini soaked in. I wondered which was the greater sin -- the butt pat from my boss or little rush it gave me -- but labeled both innocent since Alan was gay. He glanced back, pointing at his refilled glass. I nodded, ordering another. I wandered to a small bench under one of the droopy trees. I smelled the warm boxwoods, the dirt and mud and history. I tried to imagine the brilliant color of a Massachusetts autumn.

Alan sauntered back, full drinks in hand, to where I sat under a giant old branch waiting, as he suggested, for fall.

Kris Woll

LATE NIGHT RUNNERS

We've logged 120 miles since the Bradford
Pears on Grand Avenue broke into early spring.
The scent startled us out of winter lethargy
and prime time television and straight
into our running shoes. For six weeks,
we've tucked our kids in bed and left
our husbands, determined to break last
year's record, with tighter asses than ever
before. We come home around midnight,
lungs full of the sick stench of pear trees,
the insides of our thighs shaking.
We wake up with stiff calves and quiet resolve.
Twenty-four hours later, we will make
the same circle again.

Tonight, Orion's sword pierces low
from a blue-black sky over our small town,
and we meet for another late evening workout.
What I want to tell you is that you can never
run far enough. Like the beating
of his baby's heart on the ultrasound screen,
the way the whole being pulses and throbs,
heavy with his wife's blood, so you
have let him consume you, and there is no way
to cut yourself off, to escape, to sever
this cord of love or poison or sex.

But there are no words for this, only the sound
of feet hitting the pavement, music in a dance
that wards off age, cellulite, a broken marriage.
Our breath is heavy as we climb the last hill,
the last leg of our five-mile trek. We turn
heads to the ground and pump arms against
the cutting wind and the smell of blossoms
that won't ever bear fruit. Take this hill,
Miranda, you take this hill, I whisper,
though I know you won't hear me.
We stop at our cars and pencil another
entry into the log, a careful record
of a few things we can control.

Emily Hayes

WILLIAM ASHLEY PEAL

You, sir, are a cad
A rat, a bum, a fool
– no gent –
To fuck a friend – a lady –
Fuck her for your merriment!

Elegant looks, eloquent eyes
Rakish, devilish stare, yes
Dorian Gray personified when
Unzipped in your lair.

"Emotionally lazy" or a sweet
Yet troubled child? or
Toxic shame, no therapy
And too much "Girls Gone Wild?"

Dear Mister Peal, Dear Dandy Lion,
Dear Rose in cow manure,
The days and nights I'll think of you
(Praise God!)
Are growing fewer.

IT DEPENDS

Heather McAllister

> The sweat of lovers
> The breath of friends
> The much on which so much depends
>
> The politesse
> That somehow ended
> The touch on which so much depended
>
> The tearing, ripping,
> Shredding, rending
> The woven fabric of depending
>
> So feed the dog,
> Drink the wine
> There's no more hanging on this line.

Lynn Hoffman

BLACK FIRE/WHITE FIRE

(Excerpt)

Scene 4
(Eden and God together. Eden is pacing. God is holding a glass of wine.)

EDEN
God, OK. Fine, he's circumcised! But you and I know it takes a lot more than a circumcised penis for us to build a home together. My marriage proved that. I feel more jumpy than ever. Is this love? Is this it? Me, jumpy all the time. Worrying that I am falling deeper and deeper into an abyss? And where is Sophia? She has not shown up at all? Doesn't she know that I need her?

GOD
Eden, who do you think was pouring all that love out of your body in bed? Do you really think your puny little human heart could generate that much love for someone to make them cry? Really, have some humility. And give credit where credit is due. Look, clearly you're not the only one with the hots for him. Maybe, this is exactly where She wants you to be.

EDEN
I loved it. I loved the way it felt. I loved being merged and enveloped and protected and cherished and devoured. I loved it all. The rush of the passion that was beyond me.

GOD
Well, thank her, not me. I had nothing to do with it.

EDEN
What about Shakti? What if it wasn't Sophia?

GOD
Shakti, who is Shakti?

EDEN
Don't play all pious and superior with me. You know Shiva's consort...Shakti, the Divine Mother. His better half. I've been doing my homework. Sophia is not the only Goddess in town. What if it was Shakti and not Sophia who was there that night possessing me, using me! I'll never get free.

GOD
I don't move in her disco circles.

EDEN
Circles, spirals, no wonder I feel so dizzy. Out of my depth.

GOD
Eden, you look to me like a girl who is floundering and splashing around in the ocean because she doesn't know that she can swim. Eden, swim. Get your self together and start swimming in the ocean of love. You know, the Talmud obligates a father to teach his son to swim. Maybe its time a woman (points at Eden) wrote a modern commentary on the importance of mothers teaching daughters how to swim... in the ocean of love.

EDEN
Me? An expert on how to survive the shark-infested ocean of love. Me, write a romantic feminist commentary on the Talmud. This is a great idea—if I want to get my son kicked out of his religious school and me excommunicated!. Anymore, good advice?

GOD
Love thy neighbor.

EDEN
I love Van Gogh and the way I feel when I'm with his paintings. Like I'm not alone in the world.

GOD
He sounds like a soul-mate.

EDEN
Yeah, I need a man looking for a soul-mate, not a help-mate. I'm not cut-out to be Eve. Maybe I'll ask Rabbi Zohar for a blessing to find my soul-mate. He's like Van Gogh. He sees into the soul.

GOD
Eden, I may not know about love, but I know about souls. If you want to be re-united with your soul-mate, you need to start by getting re-united with your own soul.

Alana Ruben Free

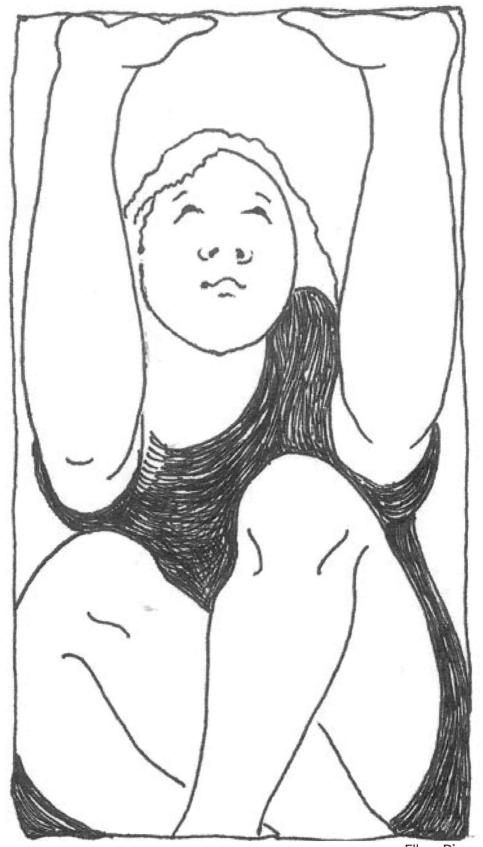

Ellen Rix

RITUAL: THE SECOND DAY IS MONDAY

for a mother alone, the kiss of dusk begins a second shift. haul flour
not water. bake bread and biscuits for the week. her words fill the
empty spaces between the lines of recipe. learn to pay them no
mind, chile. we gotta get along the best we can. between syllables,
Joshua sifts flour, holds the red knob of the gray metal sifter. the only
thing of substance he can hold onto in the kitchen. flour disappears
in a puff; reappears in his hair, on face, hands, floor, table. never
in the bowl. He sees her arms swollen from hanging the day's wet
sheets. he senses her ache. he volunteers to knead dough, watches
it rise twice, the way she does morning and night. tomorrow they will
laugh when her homemade peach preserves slide through the holes
of dough not beaten enough. still rises up, joins forces, fights back as
an army. this son, this mother, they talk survival in between the lines of
a town's recipe for know-your-place. she always tells him, remember,
the foxes is always schemin to bring ya down. but ya got to rise, son,
like yeast – rise.

SARAH'S ALTERED STATE

woman, wake up as mist rises in the morning. dip your elbow in
boiled water. the aroma of lye soap teases the hair of your nostrils,
and you become more than church usher, cook and field hand. play
that scrub board the way you play tambourine. new clothespins are
stiff, almost unbendable. in the morning become a double shift. to
replace what was lost. every woman in town wants to claim you as
her possession. before dawn, pick up a wash bin. sing to your baby
the way you used to sing to your man. then carry her on your back to
the field. pick tobacco 'til dusk calls you home to bleach linens. think
of what you lost... what you gained. a few extra coins to squirrel away
for the rain coming...

E.J. Antonio

A MY NAME IS

"A my name is Alice and my husband's name is Al, we come from Alabama and we sell Apples. Then on to B: "My name is Betty and my husband's name is Bob, we come from Boston and we sell Bananas. C my name is Carol and my husband's name is Carl we come from Carolina and we sell cats."

Even though there were few backyards in Brooklyn, we still went outside to play. We played in the street, on the stoops, the backsides of movie houses, and basement wells; discarded refrigerator boxes made great forts. The most popular girls' game of the mid-fifties was an alphabet rhyming game. All you needed was a pink Spalding High Bouncer and some good high kicking legs.

As my High Bouncer flew under my skinny long legs I would challenge my brain to come up with matching letter names of cities, husbands and merchandise. My name was Linda, I married Larry, we lived in London and sold Lettuce. My name was Peggy, I married Paul, we lived in Poughkeepsie and sold peanut butter. The aim of the game was to go from A to Z with your chant without losing control of the ball while continuing to Rockette kick without stopping in between letters. You had to recite twenty-six little operettas. The first girl to get to Z was the winner.

As I look back upon this sidewalk ritual, I can't believe my friends and I and all the girls across the Brooklyn Bridge spent hour after hour playing this hypnotic game. I now see it as a pre-feminist role determined game, focused on creating women's destiny by naming a man with whom she is attached alliteratively: I had a name, a husband a city and a job. This was the future that was mantra'd into my head, bouncing that pink ball. We were all being trained to stand by our man selling Guitars, Hats, Ice, Jam and Kettles. And it all sounded so cozy and comforting.

The only redeeming feature of the game was that I got to learn a little bit of geography. I could name places to live and sell from Antarctica to Zanzibar. I also was a real hussy--one day I would marry Gene and the next day George or Gerry. My whole life was wrapped up in this little ditty. I wouldn't go off to college. I wouldn't dance on the tables in Spain. I wouldn't read poetry with Alan Ginsberg. Everything was nailed down and sung like a lullaby, lulling me into domestic bliss.

I know it was only a silly game but we learn about ourselves from playing. Children act out their dreams and fantasies playing dress up, sports and board games. What the culture around me was condoning by having girls play "Alice" was passivity, risk aversion, conformity and deferring to others for a sense of identity. I suppose the boys weren't getting any better deal, but they weren't spinning their legs around and marrying Anna, Betty, Carla or Diane. They were off getting dirty playing ball or cowboys and Indians (that's another essay). They were swirling and diving into life, being loud and free. We never moved more than two feet from our slab of sidewalk, never sweat or argued. We were Goody--Goodies. Thank goodness the sixties was in the wings!

Lee Schwartz

I DREAMED WE HAD A MANGO TREE

And my nanny was
carrying me past it.
I asked her why we had one.
"Because they are hard
to grow here.
So it is special
if you find a good one.
Let's try," she said.
Inside, I watched her split
it and divide it into shiny,
wet sections. This woman
I never knew lifts me
And prods me to take a cube
from the skin. As I chew
the gummy pulp, I see
my mother's shadow
cross the doorway.
 "In my country," the nanny says,
"one is better than the next."
I sink my head into her
fat, black breast.
"We would never eat this one.
We would throw it out."

Wendy Levine DeVito

A LIVING WAGE

"I work 12 hour shifts at $7.00 an hour. I'm lucky I have a job."
The man was being interviewed on NPR. Hundreds had applied for
his position cleaning floors at TJ Maxx. The Bronx Borough President
was outraged that his residents were living in poverty. With a new mall
opening in Kingsbridge, every merchant would be required to pay a
living wage, which in New York City is $10 an hour with benefits, $11 an
hour without. This was considered a major victory. Were they crazy?
That's what my temp job paid, barely covering groceries and my kids'
allowance, so different from the writing commissions, and workshop
fees that I commanded not long ago

Last week, I answered an ad on Craigslist for a pre-school assistant.
I mentioned my background in educational theatre, and described
myself as a thoughtful collaborator. I've responded to hundreds of job
postings, and rarely hear back. I was excited when the director called.

"What are your salary requirements? She asked. I told her the truth. My
salaries varied depending on the job.

"We'll pay between $12 and $15 an hour."

I choked.

"Is that a problem?"
I regained my composure, focusing on healthcare and manageable
hours. We met the next morning. She was a mother of four, with
shoulder length red hair, and a heavy Long Island accent.

"I love the art on the walls, perfect as a springboard for creative
dramatics and reading comprehension," I enthused.

"Do you remember how to change diapers?" she asked.

I nodded, "Of course."
"Good. Because that's what you'll be doing – changing diapers,
and following the students around. This is an assistant's position. If the
parents ask about their children, you'll need to play dumb and refer
them to the head teacher. Do you understand?"
I have two teens, I could offer sound advice. But I knew what she
wanted to hear.

"Of course, I'll play dumb."

She showed me the sand table. "It's hard to tell by your resume how long you've been teaching. It's all mixed up with your theatre stuff."

"I appreciate your feedback. I can change that."

Silence... I continue. "The 9-2 hours work great for getting home before my kids."

She frowned. "Our children are here from 9-2. You'll be working 8:30-3:00 four days a week – and on Wednesdays you'll have to stay until 5:30."

"Forgive me, but the ad said..." The schedule was the main reason I responded.

The director was emphatic. "I was quite clear. Do you have any questions? "Can you tell me about the benefits?" Even if the pay was low at least there'd be health care.

"There are none. Every package we looked into was too expensive. However, we follow the NYC public school calendar and offer paid vacations from September through June, you'll also get three sick days." Back at her desk, I asked about the weekly salary.

She took out her calculator. "Let's say we lowball it. At $12 an hour/35 hours a week, you'd gross $420 before taxes. Are you sure this job isn't too full time for you?"
 I shook my head. "Once a month, would I be able to switch Wednesdays for another long day? I like to go to the monthly PTA meeting." My voice trailed off.
She looked at her watch.

"Can I stay and meet the kids - shadow the teachers?"

"I have several more people to interview. If we're interested, we'll call."

She stood up. We walked to the door, and she thanked me for coming in.

"Enjoy your day!" she trilled, like I was meeting friends for lunch.

No! I wanted to scream. My daughter is home sick. I need to get her medicine, and put up soup.

I thanked the director for her time. When I left I wanted to vomit. Like the worker from TJ Maxx, I'd be grateful for a weekly paycheck, even the chance to play dumb.

I phoned a friend. "I just bombed an interview. I'm not even qualified to change diapers."

"You're overqualified. They know."

Her words soothed. She was right. So was the pre-school director. This situation, like my temp job is temporary. Calmer, with a mental list of chicken soup ingredients, and ways to step up my game, I boarded the No. 7, determined not to lose hope, trusting that once again I will get paid what I'm worth, to do the work that I'm good at – to earn a real living wage.

Jessica Feder Birnbaum

LAUNDRY LESSONS

She separates darks from whites from delicates
She remembers him on her white skin
She remembers the names he calls her when he soils her
She waits quietly for the 75-cent machine by the door where she can smell fried chicken
     and waffles
The small machine perfect for her slips panties bras and the lacy blouse he gave her
She loads the jumbo washer with his blue work clothes that smell like sweat
She sets the washer for warm wash cold rinse adds heavy-duty detergent
She loads the whites checks his shorts t-shirts and white bed sheets for stains He only
     wants to sleep on white it's not easy keeping things white
She adds a little bleach to the hot water a little softener to mask the smell
One more washer for her clothes pink and yellow blouses dresses with flowers paisley
     socks every color in a crayon box
She waits outside as the wash cycles watches the superintendent sweep
She dries then folds pushes laundry home
     in a blue cart

Monica A. Hand

UNRAVELING

My infant, my daughter, my beautiful red-blond, blue-eyed child, lies in my arms, in my bed. An unseasonably cold September afternoon, raining, chill, the chill that seeps into a person's veins like formaldehyde. My three-month-old daughter sleeps in my arms; my poor, embalmed arms feel nothing.

I wrap up in the afghan I crocheted for her, the yarn I worked into granny square by square, month after pregnant month, obsessively, mathematically, finding new permutations of pastel blue, pink, yellow and green to draw through into white, infinite borders of white. I sit wrapped in yarn, unraveling.

How did I ever think I could start with yarn and crochet a garden of colors for a baby?

If only I could sleep, sleep . . .
No, study first.

Law school. How did I ever think I could get through law school with a baby at home?

A pile of case books rests on the pillow next to my infant daughter, next to markers of neon blue, pink, yellow and green, and pencils for thoughts, all for my numb hands to try to draw through into white, infinite pages of white.

Come on, just study.

Or at least color: Blue for facts (what happened in the world to cause the dispute), pink for procedural history (what happened with the case in the courts), yellow for the holding (what the court decided), green for what I can't understand.

I drift off into National Business Lists, Inc. v. Dun & Bradstreet, Inc., 552 F. Supp. 89 (N.D. 1982), sleepily coloring in facts like: "The customer does not itself receive much of the information contained in the computer data base." Feeling much like that customer, it takes me forever to get to the holding, and by that time, I've forgotten what the case was about. I'm stranded somewhere in endless fields of green.

Hoping somehow to get through the hundreds of assigned pages, I try to read cases while holding baby Freddie, nursing her, even changing her. But I swear, each time she nurses herself to sleep, she sucks more of my brain cells out with the milk. And the milk/ammonia scent? A knockout drug for those of us who've been staying up until 2 a.m. each night reading cases, and getting up again at 5 a.m. to nurse a baby-who-will-not-sleep.

Why won't she let me sleep?

By 3 a.m., I put down the books, and close my eyes. There are still endless unread pages of unintelligible heretofores, theretofores, therefors, and wherefores in every subject. If I can't get my brain back from wherever it has gone, I'll never get to my environmental law reading, where I'm already dangerously behind.

How did I ever think marking up cases in colors would somehow turn me into a lawyer?

Rose Auslander

IN THE PARLOR.

Among Hokusai prints,
stereoscopic souvenirs,
and curiosities from her grand tour
my dear aunt, Mrs. Badger,
got out her journal
and scrapbooks to reminisce
before lunch.

Warm beside the fire,
she revisited drawings, considered
the complexity of travelers and
perceptions, contemplated
Candide, the cultivation of gardens,
and her potager, covered in snow.

She culled thoughts into verse and,
as she sipped tea, read over her handiwork.
Feeling she'd rambled, she relinquished
word after word, until her poem
unraveled to a nub, the crux of her truth:

The tourist
in the garden
sees only
flowers

Lynne Shapiro

Ira Joel Haber

THE WASHERWOMAN'S DAUGHTER (1902)

(Ani, Eleven Years Old)

She beats me, prays, scalds my hand.
How she hates my hiccups and lies.
Stubborn as a gypsy child, I never cry.

All morning, she calls my name. Why
Are the laces on my boots untied?
Quick as a field rabbit I run between

the town folk's flapping sheets 'til
her hand lands, a rock against my cheek

Janet Chalmers

(74)

Take the lid off the blender while blending
And know that a splatter is pending

(44)

the wind blew my house down
so I moved into a sailboat
the wind messed my hair up
so I cut it all off
the wind made my eyes water
so I took up a collection for the sea
the wind threw the clouds out
so I threw wet cotton balls on my ceiling
the wind raised my skirt up
so I mooned it and got arrested
there was no wind in jail

(75)

scratching often switches
the location of my itches

(61)

I like my showers scalding hot
and I like to touch the lids of boiling pots of water.
lately though
I've been getting burned
I've lost a lot of my finger prints,
so I went out and bought some oven mitts
and I'm trying to adjust to my new self
the unspeakable
opposite
of invincible.

Kelli Stevens Kane

LERATO'S LULLABY

Her sister sleeps, but she must not.
Between the bolted boards, she listens for
the hiss of the Jukskei,
restless serpent of Alexandra.

Between the bolted boards, she listens for
warning shouts, torches in the shadows.
The restless serpent of Alexandra
consumed five shacks only last night.

Warning shouts, torches in the shadows --
too late to save Nonhlanhla and Siphiwe,
consumed with their shacks only last night
when the moon went blind.

Too late to save Nonhlanhla and Siphiwe,
the other children watched them float away
when the moon went blind.
Mama and Tata dreamed of a house on the hill.

The other children watched them float away
beside the hungry mud and empty bottles.
Mama and Tata dreamed of a house on the hill
to the dim drumming of the rain.

Beside the hungry mud and empty bottles,
her sister sleeps but she must not
to the dim drumming of the rain,
the hiss of the Jukskei.

Donna Katzin

AFTERNOON

You try lifting Sammy but something strong has chewed off most of his sturdy front leg, it hangs and you can see straight inside to the bone. The big dog rolls his eyes in a way that would be funny under different circumstances; then he goes to sleep forever. This is what you tell the kids: Sammy has gone to sleep forever. Buster shrieks and runs behind the juniper bush like he could catch death.

Come back here!" you shout. Not because you're insensitive, but because he has run away before, long distances, once by bus to another state. That time he got picked up by the cops and when they brought him back home he'd hung his head calling it his last chance like some old prisoner. He's only nine. You understand his need to go, and want to comfort him but there's too much blood in the grass.

"Come where I can at least see you." It's hot, and now you're bargaining with a nine year old but isn't everything like that? Even Sammy must've run down his options in that final moment of dog horror.

Wailing, Amelia drops to her knees in the grass getting blood on her shorts and long legs. Fourteen and already a beauty and doesn't she know it. You have to keep her away when the men come to pick you up for dinner or a movie. They see her and you see them getting excited. It exhausts you. But then you reason: who wouldn't get excited? Amelia has excited you, seeing her naked in the tub, despite that you've never had a woman or even wanted one.
They're not yours, but Ted's. By the time he left you'd grown used to them. Lucky them. Buster wants to follow his dad, it's there in his eyes all the time.

"Look we have to get Sammy back to the house," you say. Buster is still invisible behind the bush and Amelia is screaming, " I can't do this, don't ask me to!

You stand there next to the dead dog and think about pie crust. You wonder if ants have crawled into the flour. You left the bag open on the counter near the window with the torn screen when you heard Buster shrieking. It was intended to be an apple pie, but the boy had whined at breakfast for chocolate cream, and Amelia wanted peach. Funny how Ted never cared for pie. One less mouth to appease. And now Sammy; who'd mostly stayed under the table waiting for crumbs to fall.

Susan Tepper

This boy wears it.

You mean some calm.

He borrows the breeze from Lake Superior and sprinkles it all over his home. Look him the eye. He knows something of desire. It's the way he peals the banana, a meticulous eye on the fruit, unwrapping, golden peel by golden peel, until the naked tube of banana emerges, and with voluptuous pleasure gently gobbles it down.

It's a storm. This boy's room brews it.

A cumulonimbus cloud of balls shoot down from the ceiling – fuming. Screaming odd shapes; comported regular shapes. White, red, navy, black, and every color in between summons the unguarded intruder. It's a country you will hesitate to explore.

This boy embodies it. He is outrageously polite.

He never speaks one word to the terror sitting next to him in class for one whole year. Not even one ugly squint! They become friends the following year. "Cool Man", his first words to ex-terror-turned-friend, loaded with brio. He never tells him about covering up for him when he skips the final test because of a hangover the previous night. Neither does he hear about marks lost, nor even standing in for him in a class debate, presenting notes quickly prepared on the spur of the moment for his sake.

It's a dump. This boy's room grows it.

A spectre slinks into shape – a mountain of clothes in one corner, no, in all four corners. Yes, you see it indeed. The writing desk is discomfortingly impeccable, every item painfully set in its place – computer, monitor, speakers, accessories, and an iPod dock. Yes, the book shelf is an enigma. Each book is carefully out of place, haphazardly neat. Its charm lies in some awkward contrast in coordination.

Do you hear it? It's the cascading sound of water from the fountain hanging upside down the wall, just above the headboard. His river flows upstream, never downstream.

This boy loves his privacy.

Loud bangs ram on the bathroom door every morning from four angry siblings. He shouts back "I am thinking through it carefully, and I am surely getting there. I will be a millionaire five years after high school, a billionaire in ten. Mark it." The details of this plan neatly sprawled on a whiteboard, cover one whole wall in his room. "You are nuts", his siblings shout back in frustration. Thank God for two and half baths. Mother and father's privacy is violated. Two sisters and two brothers storm their bathroom for one whole hour.

He emerges from the bathroom two hours later exuding such rational exuberance, making him look a foot taller.

His Ford Mustang is his temple. His body is the altar. On it fancies of the mind are sacrificed.

Letters click into place,

stirs him in the face,

commands him,

jolts him to understand,

enticing,

under stupor,

the melancholy approach

executes its will,

one slap dash moment,

and it's done,

He is obsolete.

Father boxes the air in despair. Mother clasps her hands over her mouth in a painful tearful shock.

Illusions come undone; the sublime absurdity of the night.

Flora Trebi-Ollennu

on joining the navy

when the recruiter came for ma
to sign the consent forms,
I hid between the stove
exhaust pipe and the wall.

I kept my eye on her
hand curled around
the fountain pen he brought
in case she didn't have one.

the metal tip kissing the paper
with ink echoed my voice:
I'll never come back...
never come back
...never come back...

when he left, I emerged
from the space between
boy and man.

she said
nothing.

making dinner,
she stared silently
at her hand moving
beef in a current,
the sound of the
wooden spoon
around the pan
around the pan
around the pan

filling the room

Michael Haeflinger

tangerine moon (as told by *red dress*)

there is something to be said about how the tangerine moon's soft
light casts hard edged shadows across Esther's worries. her son in an
army someplace in the world she'll never see. how a land mine rips
the body to nothing. how the surviving mind becomes more twisted
than the jeep caught in its blast center. she tries hard to brush away
the paint flakes clinging to her son's freshly polished boots drying
on the windowsill. with its pale light, the moon interrupts the painful
twinges of fear, wraps her in the soothing glow of old things. the
repetitious music of her bleach-worn curtains brushing against the
window. her great-grand momma's spine-worn bible passed hand to
hand. her grand-momma's three times mended quilt. her momma's
recording of Mahalia's prayerful Come Sunday. there is something
to be said about all these loose ends of living month after month, but
she stands silent in the same exactness - spooning the moon into her
mouth.

E.J. Antonio

MISS OLIVE HOLMBERG

Clinton Hill, Brooklyn 1962

1

She believed she gave her "Christian" all, every day
This school in the middle of a struggle she knew nothing about
SNCC, Student Non-violent Coordinating Committee, sharing
     warehouse space with
The wholesale leather handbag factory on Waverly Place
She rued the day why was she chosen to serve here
The chairs in the shabby teacher's lounge
No one disputed the hierarchy of seating
Might as well have had bronze plaques soldered to their backs

The ordered pouring of slightly rusted hot water into chipped cups
I quickly learned that one did not sit at the long table uninvited
Speech specialist that I was
Relegated to a splintered chair desk against the far wall
Paint peeling, notices tacked haphazardly on faded bulletin boards
I was a peripheral, observing daily rituals
Her name conveyed peace and stiffness
No hair would dare to be out of place
Her lifetime sentence, second grade teacher

2

Reading unit on jobs and family
"What does your father do?
This Bedford-Stuyvesant neighborhood of coming and going uncles
SRO's, single moms, solid families
Street corner winos out in the noon day sun
Running their mouths at anyone and everything
Her classes had the highest scores in reading
Miss Holmberg never married
She would travel Europe when she retired
Did she expect Robin to answer
My daddy is a janitor
My daddy is a lawyer
My daddy is a dentist
My daddy is a Black Panther
Unemployed, a plumber, a junkie
I have no daddy
New charges for her to mold and
Her blessed church goings on

Births, deaths, lesson plans
She would teach them phonetics
Them lumped all her charges as one

3
Curves of newly scripted capital letters
Small index fingers bent
Little tongue tips tense
Newly mastered capital O's that looked like C's with a top curl
Learning to read from tattered picture books
White smiling Dick and Jane faces
Miss Holmberg escaped at 3 p.m. sharp
Taking the itinerant GG train from nowhere to civilization
She wouldn't dare park her shiny white Chevrolet here
The streets vibrated with architecture and life
She never noticed
Matriarch of the teacher's lunchroom
She was holding court
All her students would read by June
Be eligible to be a credit to their race
She dispensed prejudice with curriculum
Tight curls, flowered dress
"I bring a bit of spring to this wasteland", she'd say
"Paid to mold minds
I'm doing my job
God will reward me"

4
She gave that Sunday sermon
Chuckled, and shared her morning lesson
Her daddy plays with John
Doesn't that say it all about 'them"
I heard my voice silencing the room
"The John her daddy plays with is John Coltrane
Her daddy is Jimmy Garrison, the bass player"
She turned to see who dared to interrupt
Differ with her discourse
Her starched white lace handkerchief

Peeking out from a properly buttoned navy cardigan
Chest heaving- no one took on Miss Holmberg
She looked at me, disdain in the pink of her cheeks
The bell tolled the end of lunch
A quick scuffling of chairs
Chalk dust settled on crumbled waxed paper sandwich bags
She spat me a look that meant
To put me back in the second grade
Closed the door emphatically

Stand up straight when you answer
Don't forget to say yes, Miss Holmberg

Golda Solomon

EMPATHY TEST

The sun shines for only the fourth time this April,
and the light through the blinds makes perfect
stripes on the institutional tile and blue plastic
chairs. It is the second time today I have had to
ask about the Victrola in *The Glass Menagerie*,
referee arguments about whether Amanda is
pushy or Laura is (no pun intended) just lame.
Tomorrow is Tom's *El Diablo* speech, and I am
already dreading the teenaged boys who cannot
handle the line about the cathouses in the valley.
Thank God for the girl who lifts her hand and
tells the class to stop being so judgmental about
the characters because you never know how
hardships can affect a person's family, and then
I wonder why the rest of the class has not noticed
the bags under her eyes, her body wasted, thin
and fragile as a unicorn of spun glass.

Donna Vorreyer

Ira Joel Haber

LEARNING TO SAY NO

Keep your eyes open.
Place your tongue
along the roof
of your mouth
behind your front teeth.

Do not smile.

Smiles become *yes*,
stretch into *of course*,
and before you blink twice
your clothes are off
or you're cat-sitting
or buying shoes
that don't fit.

Do not smile.

Position your mouth
into a little O.
Move your tongue
forward. Release
Make a little noise.
Growl if you must.

Do not smile.

Puma Perl

RESILIENCE

for our young people

I. Your stories:

When I was 6 years old I rode the subways listening to the wind and wheels scraping and screeching against the metal tracks---the soundtrack to the craziness in my family.

They pinned me to the ground, four of them, each holding down a limb; then I blacked out.

I'm hungry. I'm always hungry. There's never enough food for all of us. I eat as little as possible so there's more for the others. I eat the bones.

I said, "No", and then he raped me.

His face exploded with blood splattering all over me, the doctors, nurses, the white walls of the ER. I heard screaming and realized it was me.

We live in the back room of a store and have to be quiet as mice or we'll be thrown out--- homeless on the street.

My teacher said, How can you write poetry? You write poetry? in a mean voice and she said it in front of the class and some of the kids laughed. I still hear them laughing.

There are days I can't get up, can't get up, drowning in this too heavy world; so I sleep and sleep, and sleep.

Because I play basketball all the time and don't like to use make up or get dressed up the kids call me gay. Even my mother's asking me all the time and saying what's wrong with you; and then she makes me go out with her friends' sons. I hate it.

What if we get kicked out of this country---we're make believe people with fake papers and make believe names.

She has these crazy moods and starts beating us for being bad, disrespectful, for looking at her the wrong way and she grabs anything--- wire hanger, stick, slippers, her hands, there's always her hands balled up in a fist.

They always told me I was stupid, why so slow and clumsy tripping over my own feet.

I woke up with a pillow shoved into my face. I can't breathe. Can't breathe. I can't breathe. I couldn't push him off. His full weight was on me, I lost consciousness; and then when I woke up I thought, Was that a dream?

I'm like Cinderella: minding all the younger children, so many younger children! Washing, cooking, feeding, bathing, oh so many chores without time for my self; never allowed to go anywhere with anyone outside of the family.

They wonder why I don't talk. I watch and don't say anything because what's the use.

Subway tracks, bridges, tops of buildings call me to leap and fly. Frozen in one spot I break into a cold sweat.

Stole his bottle, stole his smokes, stole his pills and still it hurts all over.

I scratch myself till I bleed and pick the sores till I feel nothing. My girl friend cuts her self. We're in the school bathroom and no one knows. No one.

My father has cancer. My brother has cancer. The house smells like death. Pain is silent.

I am cold.

I am hungry.

I can't get anywhere.

The world is too big.

No money for food.

No money for bus or subway.
  I walk for miles.

No money for shoes
  or warm boots.

No winter coat,
  a clean shirt.

No money for books.

No home.

104

II.   Still you say,
          Yes.

Yes, with open hearts,
       smiling eyes
       bright and eager

You want to
        finish school
        find a job
        find a place to call
            home
        be independent
        travel and have adventures
        be grown up
        have good friends
        and some day your own family.

You want a chance.

III. So,
        still you sing
        still you dance
        still you open your arms
              wide to possibility and
        your resilience
             stills me
               fills me with hope
              for good
                in this world.

Fay Chiang

[string search: "mother" and "memory" and "mine"]

> When all the involved calculations prove false, and the
> philosophers themselves have nothing more to tell us,
> it is excusable to turn to the random twitter of birds. . .
> --Marguerite Yourcenar

Katzenjammer Kids   She sipped the cup of wisdom
Man Mountain Dean   from Joyce Brothers—

He'll always be your father   We treated her as slightly
A watched pot never boils   addlepated—

I'll fix your wagon, buster   she said later, handing
Take someone out to lunch   me a ten dollar bill—

A generation of vipers   At six I was ashamed—
Roué, mañana, cad   Years go fast, days no.

    The New Yorker was her talisman against
       the stupefying California sun.

*

She made   the trip   to Jerusalem   alone   to see   her daughter.
(Dad refused to fly   or post-Achille Lauro   cross by water.)

*

   Up late,   I buttonhole   a pulsing cursor

     and trawl for time retrieved. I close
my eyes. . .

    Desert Hospital, dementia, cards unread.
Her eldest sister gently said, *Lucille, do you know who I am?*

You're the boss, she answered brightly, *You're the boss.*

   - The Mother of All Labor Day Sales
   - White Goddess, a Moderated Chat

    Did you mean: <u>smother</u>

klipschutz

Ira Joel Haber

TOOTHSOME

In her thirties, Nellie wore miniskirts and go-go boots, false eyelashes and hairpieces, and seemed oh so with it, up-to-date, and modern. Her small square teeth gleamed in a perfect line behind a red lipstick mouth. She laughed and giggled, weak in the knees, through days where nickel and dime tips forestalled economic disaster. Her life was hard work and more work and raising kids, and sexual trysts on the sly. Nothing long-standing, nothing lasting.

Even the children metamorphosed into upwardly mobile wraiths who disappeared, then reappeared with babies. But Nellie was strong, looked younger than her age, and there were her teeth. Perfect. She had no cavities.

In her fifties, she finally needed dental work. Nellie traveled to Juarez, Mexico to get the work done cheap. The dentist suggested gold fillings for three of her front teeth. He patted her knee. "Special price for you."

Her children had only seen gold teeth on winos and the occasional rap music star. "Why?" they asked each other in disbelief.

Nellie shrugged. "He said gold would last forever." She flashed her golden smile often, and the kids gave her $500 to get the gold taken out. Nellie bought a new water heater instead. "I look fine," she said, "you try taking a shower in ice cold water and see how you like it."

In her seventies, her teeth began to trouble her. They would have to be removed. "Give her the best dentures available," her children told the dentist, secretly relieved that the gold-lined teeth would go. Nellie would look like every other senior citizen equipped with porcelain choppers.

"Don't let the dentist keep that gold," Nellie warned her children when they took her for the surgery. "I paid a pretty penny for it!"

"Everyone wants their teeth blazing white these days," her children told her. "You'll look modern."

Nellie frowned. "I don't want people to know I'm wearing false teeth. Makes you look old."

The dentist fitted her dentures perfectly to her mouth and handed her a mirror. Nellie smiled at her reflection, turning her head to the right and the left. She ran her tongue over her small square teeth gleaming in a perfect line and nodded at the dentist, satisfied.

Her children waited in the lounge and stood to greet her as she left the office. She gave the dentist a hug. "You're a genius!" she gushed, "I look better than ever."

Nellie turned, and smiled wide at her sophisticated children, gold now lining every single artificial tooth in her mouth.

Sandra Ramos O'Briant

STUFFED ARTICHOKES

Naturally there will be food.
I call my mother long distance
and after the Happy Easter's
she will tell me what she's fixed
for the family down there.
The usual turkey and oyster dressing,
a spinach and chick pea casserole,
French green beans, and, ah,
stuffed artichokes. Suddenly
I must have them, it's been so long.
My mother cooks by instinct,
by religion, but I coax the recipe
out of her anyway, knowing
that I will have to decipher
into more precise terms, those
of an auditor or accountant,
more directive, less magic.
Well, she laughs, it's easy,
and repeats the old story:
a secret recipe handed down
from some great-grandmother
who sold ravioli in the streets
of Genoa. First, she says, chop
up a bulb of garlic and a pile
of flat leaf parsley . . . a whole bulb?
that's a lot of garlic, I'm thinking . . .
and add about half a container
of grated Romano and parmesan,
oh, and the same amount of bread crumbs,
the Italian kind from Progresso.
Put them in a pan with about an inch
of water and douse the tops with olive oil--
don't forget to cut off the stems
and points at the top. Spread the leaves
with your fingers and stuff it in.
That's it . . . let them steam.
How long? I ask. Until you can
pick the leaves off tenderly.
Do it on a low to medium flame.
Tenderly. That's a lot of garlic,
I finally sigh.

She laughs, it's for eight people, what
you thought it was just one artichoke?
I'll have to try it, I tell her, certain now
I will never try, that at some point
I will burn the leaves, add too many
bread crumbs, go slightly higher
on one cheese or the other, use
the wrong olive oil. Tenderly.
I cannot hope to watch the leaves
detach themselves and rise
from the pot like angels.
My faith is neither enviable
nor extravagant. I hope you do,
she says, pleased, mother happy,
but remember, the recipe is a secret.
Don't tell anybody.

Louis Gallo

EVA

Survived Hitler
Wears a baseball cap
Her hair like silver filaments.

Talks about her Czech days
Eyes electric
Voice sharp as broken glass.

Says she was a seamstress
Says she was a model
Says she slept at Harvard
When her son was a student

Says she loves my mother,
Who looks like her *maminka*
Smiles at us
my mother dozing in her chair.

Nancy Gerber

LESSONS

In her cabbage-flowered housecoat she holds
the silver canister beneath her heart,
to toss a fist full of leaves into the Delft pot, then
douses them with boiling water.
"You have to let it seep," she says.
Her hands round the Blue Willow
cup painted with two Chinese lovers
plotting on a wooden bridge, she mostly listens.
Then she tips my drained cup:
in the leaves a black-haired man
I will someday marry and the blood-red boat
we will sail on in and out of seas
and over weeks and years. It is good
to wait and to be silent.
Tranquility has granted her ninety-six years
and when, near the end, her lungs bloated with fluid,
a nurse serves her piss-yellow tea not fit for pigs,
in the leaves a howling wolf,
she turns her cup upside down
and sets its rim in the round lip of the saucer.

Liz Dolan

BERGEN MERCY

Claiming a city. Collecting signs.
I am back to say goodbye.

Tidyland
Laundromat.

Associated Thrift:
Yesterday's Best.

"Jan"-tiques. Owner Jan Gardner.
A trip to the past with a touch of class.

Blood pressure 126 over 90.
72nd and Dodge. Heritage Village.

New Lady Fitness. Suburban Bridals.
From Here to Maternity.

NW Radial Hwy in Benson.
Omaha Lace Laundry. A fashion cleaner.

Musette Bar. Grampy's Odds & Ends.
All proceeds go to Uta Hallee Home for Girls.

Tip Top Thrift Shop.
Jim's Seek & Save.

Enter Through Alley. Buy an antique
that evokes a favorite memory

of a special person in your life
or a happy occasion from your childhood.

My mother sat on the gossip bench
talking to Aunt Honey on the rotary dial.

I walked past,
rubbing sleep out of my eye.

Thinking I was sad, my mother
pulled me onto her lap to comfort me.
Because I didn't want her to stop,
I pretended to cry.

Animal Ark Shelter.
Return to Willoughby.

Please come browse,
I know you will find

that perfect memory
to take home.

James Cihlar

what i wanted to do for my mother

was to hold her in my arms and sing to her whisper that she would be
all right that she was safe that i would take care of her that i would
take her home soon where she could cook her own oatmeal the
way she liked it home where she could stay up all night reading if she
wanted to home where she planned to celebrate her ninety-eighth
birthday going up in a hot air balloon except i could not hold her as
she was in too much pain and cried at even the slightest touch so i
sang and whispered and promised and she called me mama as she
lay dying i did not correct her because long ago we made up little
plays where i was the mother and she was the little girl and this was no
different except now i was the only one who knew it was a play.

Marcia Popp

NOTHING TO DO WITH DIONYSUS

Instead of going to my dying mother's bed,
I write an inconstant poem
for her. What reason? What is it
I am?
If you drink out the sun, if
your tongue is scald forever,
the pain must form on something

the form of which saves you.
Because in ancient Greece the actors left the stage
to switch their masks and voices,
a chanting chorus covered the changes,
they say. I say
the art of the sons and daughters
is all that holds us,

crossing, re-crossing, treading out tragedy.
One dance across the stage becomes
one line of a poem, the verse
where the dancers turn.
Millennia pass.
A sadness without myth climbs into the lines
as into a lap.

Between the stanzas
the mothers are inconsolable.
If the words do not turn and call us back
the poems break out
and dance up into the mountains,
their feet moving under the snow.

Mary Harter Mitchell

I plumb my mother.

These are all imaginings.

I fist into hard-ridged canals lined with dark pink membrane.

I do not feel her pain.

Many urchin valves open swiftly.

There is no location.

Periodically, maroon clots, black clots, flit past my fingers.

I am not able, in the end, to hold onto anything.

I see veins of blood against light-infused flesh.

I am too conscious.

I pass through, that is all; no blood touches me.

I am not reborn.

Ana Silva

Mother,

When I thought the light had left me, it was you
who had me swallow chains

of mirrors to reveal fire rippling across bramble.
My interior—waves of heat

moving where I snapped my bones for kindling.
It was you

who clawed out from that husk of gossamer
to put my collar

bone back on—taught me I was more than
broken. We are more

than our mistakes. You made / unmade,
and from the raveling /

unraveling you wove a tapestry
of women passing

the stone of memory—hand
to hand—bridging

generations. You are not
the drugs. You are

who stands despite
their arm-sized cords—

you who knows life
is granted daily—

through you I am
born again, again,

again. In a
gathering
of light.

Nicelle Davis

FIRST NIGHT IN THE CABIN, NEW YEAR, PROUST, MY MOTHER

Because the fire is elemental
And sheltering night is calm
I am warm inside my cabin
On my first night lived within it
Reading Proust both for my students
And my mother
Facing a less delicious darkness
Facing a night that never darkens
But stays streaked like a mist, like twilight
Perpetual and unrelenting---
That's the pain---and because sleep
Will come more slowly or not at all---
I will bring her to my cabin
To the fire, elemental
To the night that settles darkly
To the quiet and the comfort
We'll talk, as usual, about politics
And then Proust, that he seems
A little boy but is middle-aged and sick
On the first night of his book
A night perpetual, relentless
Made of waiting for a kiss.

Cynthia Kraman

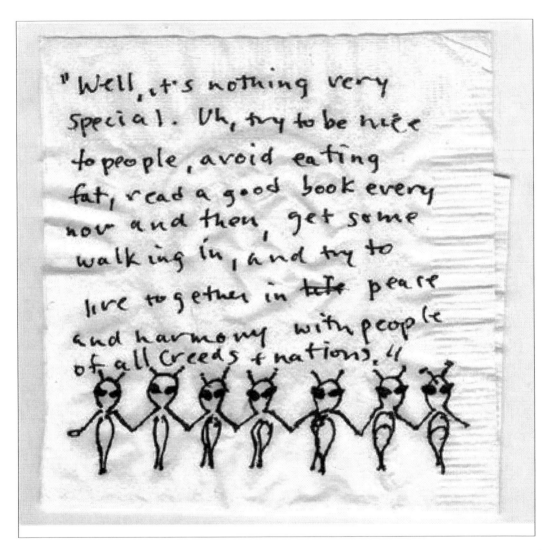

"Well, it's nothing very special. Uh, try to be nice to people, avoid eating fat, read a good book every now and then, get some walking in, and try to live together in peace and harmony with people of all creeds & nations."

Mary Reilly

THE VISIT

Yesterday marked five years since my stepfather, Dougie, passed away. My eighty-two-year-old mother hasn't visited him in the cemetery much, preferring to honor and connect with him through happy memories in her mind and photographs. Visiting the burial plot just isn't her thing, she's told me.

"But, it's the right thing to do," she said about her plan to visit his plot on the five-year anniversary. "I want him to see that I'm still making it. Still standing, and that you're there with me."

The day was warm, typical for this time of year in Los Angeles, bringing out lots of visitors to the Westwood Memorial Cemetery. It's a small cemetery hidden from view and tucked away behind a movie theatre and a stone's throw from the busiest intersection in LA many of the local residents don't even know it exists.

My mother and I made our way down the narrow driveway which leads to the entrance of the cemetery grounds - an entrance that's anything but impressive given such occupants as Marilyn Monroe, Jack Lemmon, Armand Hammer and Natalie Wood, to name a few.

We drove past the small administration building and parked on the side closest to Dougie's plot.

I helped Mom from the car. She's moving a little slower these days. Parkinson's has crept into her life since Dougie passed away, but she's taking it on like she does most things – with humor and a gritty determination to keep it under control. Once lazy and prone to put things off, she exercises daily now. "Even if it's pushing the market cart up and down the aisles for twenty minutes," she says, "I've gotta do it every day or I'm screwed."

Medication plus a healthier diet has proved well for her, and although she's not running and jumping, she's hanging in there.

"Look," Mom said as she walked across the grounds. "Look who is just steps away from Dougie."

I read the headstone. Farrah Fawcett.

"Poor beautiful thing," Mom remarked. "Damn that cancer."
We moved over to the wall in the "Garden Gated Estates" where

Dougie's ashes are interned. His plot is on the top. Mom's plot will be under him. The four plots below are blank. I smiled remembering when Enid, the "Sales Associate," and now my mother's good friend, had tried to sell the plots below to my husband, Hank, and me.

"Mom," I'd protested, "Hank would die if his ashes were below you and Dougie! There'd be no eternal rest for us with you both above."

My mother stood looking up at his plot. Her face grew somber. "How old would he be today?" she asked, trying to figure the dates.

"Ninety-two."

A middle-aged man with a camera brushed past with two women in tow. One was carrying a map of the cemetery. "Over here," he said, "Fanny Brice."

"Wait!" cried the woman holding the map, "We missed Eve Arden!"

I looked over to the right. Another threesome was taking a picture of Marvin Davis' tomb.

"Let's walk around," I said. "We'll come back when these tourists thin out."

We moved over to another wall close by and I pointed out Alice's plot, the mother of a close friend of mine. A lovely lady, Alice was, I tell Mom. She knitted sweaters and blankets for the poor.

"Does she play bridge?" Mom asked. "Dougie would love that."

Mom checked out some plots on the ground, the tips of her false eyelashes touched the lenses of her glasses as she looked down. "So many more famous people have come since we bought our plots," she said. "Dougie must be beside himself. He loved mixing with high profile people."

Scanning names and dates on the wall, I reminded Mom of the day she and Dougie bought their burial plots six years ago. "Do you remember when he tried to get a discount on your plots because he'd already bought one next to his third wife and he didn't want to be laid to rest next to her anymore?"

Mom laughed. "Oh, god. Enid's face! It took a few minutes for her to respond. Finally she said, 'Well, Mr. MacDougall, we've never actually had anyone ask for discount because they've changed their mind and want to be next to someone else instead.'"

We walked a little further around some small bubbly stone fountains. "He died the same weekend that Rodney Dangerfield died, remember, Mom?"

"How can I forget," she said. "The day Dougie was interned they were setting up for a big service that night for Rodney. Sparkly lights, tented and everything. Right here in the cemetery. Dougie always loved a party."

The people with the map moved on and Mom and I went back to Dougie. I studied her as she stood and looked at his plot. She's little more stooped these days, but still wearing the bright orange long fingernails, the false lashes, and the bubble hairdo. She still covers her lips with Revlon's "Crystal Cut Coral" and she still loves to talk on the phone.

She reached up to touch the little plaque marking his plot. "Bye, Dougie. Love you."

Back at the car, I opened door and helped her back in. "You know what?" she said, seated now, looking up at me and reaching for her seatbelt.

I held the door open. "What, Mom?"

"I'm thinking that I want 'Ciao Bella' on my plaque."

Heather Haldeman

LEGACY

In the mirror
heredity grins, it cracks
at the mouth
clutches at the corners
of my eyes.

Is it me in her
or her in me?

We don't discuss it.
She gets older,
I *mature*,
and we move like one dancer
in a time-worn mirror.

My laughter is hers
but the jokes are my own,
as are my hands
& what I do with them.

Traitor that I am,
I collect her silences
& put them into words,
creating poems instead of children.

Will she forgive
my dark sense of humor,
these wicked fingers
that hammer her life?

Try as I might
to enclose myself in silence,
I hear heredity titter
& taunt me with her laughter.

Mindy Kronenberg

RECIPE TO AVOID HATE

The recipe to avoid hate isn't complex. A few basic
ingredients: clean water, food, shelter, sweaters,
and daily hugs. Add generous spoonfuls of humor,
compassion for broken spirits, respect for the co-existence
of insects. Cultivate the seedlings of self-love with care.
Upon dark occasion, sprinkle with red pepper
and pour pure maple syrup thickly when sour.
Cut open ginger root or splash lemon juice
wherever melancholy hits. Shut your eyes and hum
a little made-up tune if Teacher belittles you in front
of class and later in life when Boss dismisses you
with the flick of her wrist, go to the Internet and look up
the nesting habits of hermit crabs. The most important thing
to experience after that pink-faced woman in her white SUV
has attempted to gun you and your son down as you crossed
the street for the park—besides midsummer rainfall and its lush
green light—is lifting your face to the sky with your son held
tightly in your arms. Look beyond rainclouds to the red orange
flare of your soul. Be thankful you live to love.

Rebecca Dosch-Brown

LOVE YOUR BROTHER

"You've got to have love
for your brother,"
his daddy told him.
"I did,"
he replied.
"But it keeps getting smaller."

We, the parents, pause.
We are struck by his honesty
and the logic
in this statement.

"You need to get it back,"
we tell him,
not even sure ourselves
of how to do this.

Haydn nods his head
seriously.
He stares as his daddy talks
to his brother.
A moment passes,
and he says,
"It's back."

Heather Truett

ONE TRUE THING

This is what I know:
even in this world,
there is loveliness real enough
to lift the old doors from their hinges -

there are places where the land remains
untouched, where late summer hangs low
above a raspy field, where morning light
is enough to lift the prayer, however simply spoken.

Once, an olive tree
held my imagination for days,
making up for several years
of useless fretting. So I ask you:

what lifts your soul? Whatever its name,
it wants your attention. It is
what you were made for, and nothing else
will ever suffice.

Allison Elrod

LISA ARGRETTE AHMAD *Resistance* is part of a collection of mini-memoirs Lisa is writing about her twenty-year marriage to a Pakistani-American, Muslim man. She is African-American and was Christian until the day she married. The author is a graduate of Wellesley College and the Harvard Business School. She lives outside New York City with her husband and three children.

E.J. ANTONIO is a 2009 fellow in Poetry from the New York Foundation for the Arts and a recipient of fellowships from the Hurston/Wright Foundation and the Cave Canem Foundation. Her work has been published in various Journals and magazines, most recently, *Black Renaissance/Renaissance Noire*, and *Mobius: The Poetry Magazine*. Her work is forthcoming in *The Encyclopedia Project*. Her first chapbook, *Every Child Knows*, was published in the Fall of 2007 by the Premier Poets Chapbook Series, and she is one of the featured poets on the CD, *Beauty Keeps Laying Its Sharp Knife Against Me: Brant Lyon and Friends*.

"Unraveling" is an excerpt from ROSE AUSLANDER'S memoir-in-progress, *Pencils on the Ceiling*. The shortest version is her six-word memoir: "Mathematician's daughter -- has trouble counting." She is Poetry Editor of Folded Word Press, and a lawyer, but stays away from math. Her work has appeared in *Referential Magazine, Form.Reborn* (winning a Three Cheers award), *Conversation Magazine, PicFic* and *Short, Fast, and Deadly*. Her great, great uncle, Joseph Auslander, was the first Poet Laureate of the United States, and she hopes to make him proud, wherever he may be. And she blogs! http://www.rausland.wordpress.com

RADHIYAH AYOBAMI is a 2006 Fiction Fellow with the New York Foundation of the Arts, and a Cave Canem Fellow. She has been published in the *Chicago Sun-Times, Bowery Women: Poems*, and *TwentySomething Essays by TwentySomethingWriters: The Best New Voices of 2006*. She is currently blogging on Facebook about her experiences as a financially challenged mama and writer navigating the maze of housing, education and social services in the city of New York. A lifelong student of writing, African history, natural childbirth, veggie food, and religion, she loves dance class, poems that heal, the beach, and her eleven year old son.

ROBYN BEATTIE's photography show "Hidden worlds--A closer look at tiny treasures" debuted in the Graton Gallery in Sonoma County, California, summer 2009. One of five children raised by Bohemian parents in the Healdsburg redwoods, Robyn writes, "I see my art as a form of archaeology, digging amongst the stuff of life to find those small gem-like segments, revealing these tiny, close-up worlds." http://www.robynbeattie.com.

Mom to one, KIMBERLY L. BECKER is a member of Wordcraft Circle of Native Writers and Storytellers. Her poetry appears widely, in journals and anthologies. Finalist for the DeNovo Award (C&R Press), recipient of a grant from the Arts and Humanities Council of Montgomery County (MD), she is adapting Cherokee myths into plays for Cherokee Youth in Radio.

Artist ORNA BEN- SHOSHAN creates metaphysical paintings that infuse deep spiritual experience with subtle humor. She conceives the images she paints through channeling Orna has been an autodidact artist for the past 30 years. Her artwork was exhibited in numerous locations in the USA, Europe and Israel. website: http://www.ben-shoshan.com. "Kabbalah Insights" website present various products for personal guidance based on her visionary artwork and kabbalah symbols: http://kabbalah.ben-shoshan.com .

LAURIE BILLMAN grew up in Colorado and many of her poems are inspired by the West. She now lives in North Carolina with her husband, an anthropologist, and two teenage daughters, more fodder for her creative work. She works as a mental health therapist. Her poetry has appeared in *The McGuffin, 13th Moon, Seedhouse, CHEST, San Pedro River Review*, and *The Rambler*, and in the anthologies *Not What I Expected, Night Whispers*, and *Sand and Sea*.

GRETA BOLGER is a mother, grandmother, writer, photographer and entrepreneur from Michigan. She has been published in print and online journals, including *Thema, Raven Chronicles, The Chimaera, Third Coast, Juice Box*, and elsewhere. Motherhood is the crucible through which she has learned much, suffered much, and gained compassion for all women everywhere who take on the life-long, no-guarantees responsibility of being someone's mom. Its rewards are well deserved.

CHERYL BOYCE-TAYLOR lives in New York City; she works as a teaching artist and Social Worker in NYC. Her poems have previously appeared in *The Mom Egg, Pank, To Be Left With The Body* and the *Naugatuck River Review*, to name a few. In January 2010 Cheryl graduated from Stonecoast University of Southern Maine MFA program with a degree in Poetry.

RONDA BROATCH is the author of Shedding Our Skins, (Finishing Line Press, 2008), and Some Other Eden, (2005). Nominated several times for the Pushcart, Ronda is the recipient of a 2007 Artist Trust GAP Grant, and her manuscript, *Rib of New Fruit*, was a finalist for the 2009 May Swenson Poetry Book Award. She is currently an assistant editor for Crab Creek Review.

ELIZABETH-JANE BURNETT is an interdisciplinary poet with a focus on experimental writing and performance. She studied English at Oxford University, Poetic Practice MA at Royal Holloway, University of London, Applied Poetics in New York, Performance Writing at Naropa, Colorado, and is currently completing a PhD in Contemporary Poetics at Royal Holloway. Forthcoming chapbooks include *slam poems for quiet people* and *Exotic Birds* www.elizabethjaneburnett. com.

SARAH WERTHAN BUTTENWIESER is a graduate of Hampshire College & the MFA for Writers Program at Warren WIlson College. A former reproductive rights organizer/educator, she writes about women, motherhood, the arts & more. Her work has appeared on *Literary Mama, Mamazine, & Mothers Movement Online*, in *Brain Child, Family Fun* and *Ars Medica*, amongst others & in anthologies, most recently *The Maternal is Political* (Seal Press) edited by Shari MacDonald Strong. She lives in Northampton, Massachusetts, with her husband, four children & zero pets. Her blog, Standing in the Shadows, is at http://www.valleyadvocate.com/blogs/ standingintheshadows.

ROSALIE CALABRESE is a native New Yorker whose poetry has appeared in *Cosmopolitan, Poetry New Zealand, Poetica, Jewish Currents, Jewish Women's Literary Annual, ByLine, Möbius, The Mom Egg, And Then, Thema* and several other publications, including anthologies. She also writes short stories and books and lyrics for musicals.

LUZ CELENIA lives in Rockland County with her husband and three children. She spends her time supporting the arts, working for a local family support organization and building her professional organizing business. She dedicates this to her own mother, the most amazing warrior mom she's ever known. http://warrior-mom.blogspot.com

JANET CHALMERS, a New York writer and photographer, is currently working on a series of linked poems called *Diamonds & Toads: An Invention In Two Parts*. She has an MFA from Columbia University and has written political and social commentary for many publications in the US and Mexico, as well as poems and reviews for *Inkwell, Barrow Street, The Kenyon Review* (online), *Mamapalooza, The Mom Egg* and *Chelsea*.

FAY CHIANG is a poet and visual artist who believes culture is a spiritual and psychological weapon used for the empowerment of people and communities. Working at Project Reach (www.projectreach.org), a youth center for young people at risk in Chinatown/Lower East Side, she is also a member of Zero Capital, a collective of artists (www.zerocapital.net); the Orchard Street Advocacy and Wellness Center, which supports people affected by HIV/AIDS, cancer and other chronic illnesses. Battling her 8th bout of breast cancer, she is completing *Chinatown*, a book-length poem and a memoir. *Seven Continents 9 Lives* was recently released by Bowery Press.

JAMES CIHLAR's book, *Undoing*, was published by Little Pear Press: http://littlepearpress.com. The Books Review Editor for *American Poetry Journal,* he also reviews for the *Minneapolis Star Tribune* and *Coldfront*. Winner of a Minnesota State Arts Board Fellowship and a Glenna Luschei Award from *Prairie Schooner*, Cihlar lives in St. Paul.

DENISE EMANUEL CLEMEN's publications include the *Georgetown Review, Two Hawks Quarterly & Literary Mama.* She's received fellowships to The Virginia Center for the Creative Arts, Vermont Studio Center, Ragdale, and was a fellow at *Moulin á Nef* in France in '09. Denise has a completed memoir manuscript & a novel in progress. She is a blogaholic: http://www.hisbigfatindianwedding.blogspot.com, http://deniseemanuelclemen.blogspot.com/ & http://myfrenchunderpants.blogspot.com/

JULIE CLINE is a stay at home mom (hah!) who spends her free time managing investments, driving a cab, running a laundry service and catering 3-4 meals daily. In the wee hours while suffering insomnia she writes. She is still learning lessons from her very smart children.

NICELLE DAVIS lives in Southern California with her husband James and their son J.J. Her poems are forthcoming in *Caesura, FuseLit, Illya's Honey, Moulin, The New York Quarterly, Redcations,* and *Transcurrent.* She'd like to acknowledge her poetry family at the University of California, Riverside and Antelope Valley Community College. She runs a free online poetry workshop at: http://nicelledavis.wordpress.com/.

WENDY LEVINE DEVITO lives in Hartsdale, NY with her husband and two young children. Her poem "Orlando" appeared in *The Mom Egg 09 Online Edition.* Her work has also appeared in *Literary Mama, The Ampersand Review,* and *Poetica.* She teaches English.

LIZ DOLAN's first poetry collection, *They Abide,* has been published by March Street Press. A five time Pushcart nominee, Liz has won a 2009 fellowship as an established professional from the Delaware Division of the Arts. In addition, a yet to be published manuscript, *A Secret of Long Life,* has been nominated for the Robert McGovern Prize, Ashland University. She has also been published in *On the Mason Dixon Line: An Anthology of Contemporary Delaware Writers,* U of DE Press. Most recently she received an honorable mention in creative non-fiction from the DDOA, 2010. Currently, she serves on the poetry board of *Philadelphia Stories.* She lives with her husband in Rehoboth Beach. Her nine grandchildren live one block away.

REBECCA DOSCH-BROWN lives *in media res* in Minnesota with her husband, an electronica composer, and their bright son, whose name means 'sun' in Japanese. She is a teacher of creative writing, EFL, and cultural awareness. She also has enjoyed stints as a gardener for rich people, a translator of modern Japanese poetry, and served as an apprentice in modern bonsai and tile-making.

R. H. DOUGLAS is a diarist, performance artist and storyteller. Her work has been published in anthologies and literary journals, including: *Life Notes; Patchwork of Dreams; Erotique Noire; Pearls of Passion; In Praise of African American Mothers; Creation Fire* and *New Voices.* She has conducted writing workshops for senior citizens through Poets & Writers. RH has performed at several venues, as an individual and with her performance group, SpiritWoman.

ALLISON ELROD is a poet and essayist whose work draws deeply on her love of plain language and ordinary life. Her essays have appeared in *The Living Church* and on Charlotte's National Public Radio station, WFAE. Her poems have been recognized by the Randall Jarrell Poetry Competition and the Poet Laureate Contest of the North Carolina Poetry Society. Her recent work is included or forthcoming in *Kakalak, an Anthology of Carolina Poets, Iodine Poetry Journal* and *Cave Wall.* She is an associate editor at Lorimer Press in Davidson, North Carolina.

ELIZABETH ENSLIN received a 2009 Individual Artist Fellowship award from the Oregon Arts Commission and is currently finishing an ethnographic memoir on her experiences as anthropologist and mother in Nepal. Recent work appears in *The Gettysburg Review, Crab Orchard Review, Opium Magazine, Fringe Magazine, The Truth About the Fact, The Smoking Poet, High Desert Journal,* and *Oregon Literary Review.* She divides her time between a house in Portland and a yurt in northeastern Oregon. Learn more at www.elizabethenslin.com.

KATHRYN M. FAZIO is a mother engaging in literary activism. She is winner of the First Ed Rehberg Prize for poetry naming her poet laureate of the College of Staten Island, C.U.N.Y. She is a recipient of the Silla Gold Crown World Peace Literature Prize, and represented the U.S.A. at the 5th World Congress of Poets for Poetry Research and Recitation.

JESSICA FEDER-BIRNBAUM is a playwright, teaching artist, non-fiction writer, licensed tour guide, real estate agent and mother of two teens. She is lyricist and librettist for a biographical musical, entitled 'Margaret Sanger: A Woman Rebel,' for which a July 2010 reading is slated at the Richmond Shepard Theatre in New York City. She is creator/founder of the multi-generational MAMAPALOOZA family event and proud to serve on MAMAPALOOZA's board of directors.

Born in Port-au-Prince, Haiti, M.J. FIEVRE is the author of several mystery novels and children's books in French; her latest include *Le Fantôme de Lisbeth* and *Les Fantasmes de Sophie*. Her short stories and poems have appeared in literary journals, such as *P'an Ku* and *Healthy Stories*. M.J. holds a B.S. in Education from Barry University. She's presently a graduate student in the Creative Writing program at Florida International University and working on a memoir. M.J. is the secretary of Women Writers of Haitian Descent, Inc.

ALANA RUBEN FREE is a playwright (The Eden Trilogy), poet (*Bowery Women*), performer ("Beginner at Life)", and writer (*The Mom Egg*). She was founding editor of *The Mom Egg* and is the producer of the documentary, "The Last Stand". Her play, "Beginner at Life", is currently in production in Australia, Israel and Italy. "Fear and Desire" was showcased at last year's ARM/Mamapalooza conference and coming to Australia, May 2010. "Love Thy Stranger" had its first reading in NYC in February, 2010. http://www.beginneratlife.com.

LOUIS GALLO teaches English at Radford University, Virginia. His work has appeared in *Glimmer Train, American Literary Review, Missouri Review, New Orleans Review, The Ledge, storySouth, Raving Dove* (Pushcart nominee), *Rattle, Baltimore Review, Portland Review, Greensboro Review* and many others.

NANCY GERBER is the author of *Portrait of the Mother-Artist: Class and Creativity in Contemporary American Fiction* (Lexington, 2003) and *Losing a Life: A Daughter's Memoir of Caregiving* (Hamilton, 2005). She is grateful to the mother-artists of The Mom Egg community for their support of her work.

GAIL GHAI's poetry has appeared in *Descant, JAMA, Kaliope, Poet Works, Shenandoah* and Yearbook of American Poetry. Her awards include a Pushcart Prize nomination, a Henry C. Frick scholarship for creative teaching and a travel scholarship from the Pittsburgh Center for the Arts. Her Color Thesaurus poster, "Painted Words" can be found @ www.artpoetica.com.

JANLORI GOLDMAN received an MFA in poetry from Sarah Lawrence College, where she had the good fortune to work with Tom Lux and Laure-Anne Bosselaar. She has also studied with Jean Valentine, Brenda Shaughnessy, and Ilya Kaminsky. Janlori has a poem in the Spring 2010 issue of *The Cortland Review*, and was a semi-finalist for the 2009 Lois Cranston Memorial Award in Poetry from *Calyx: A Journal of Art and Literature by Women*. For over 25 years, Janlori has been a civil liberties and health advocate. She teaches at the School of Public Health at Columbia University, and lives in New York City with her teenage daughter.

IRA JOEL HABER is a sculptor, painter, book dealer and teacher. His work has appeared in group shows in the US and Europe, and he has had nine one-man shows including several retrospectives of his sculpture. His work is in the collections of The Whitney Museum Of American Art, New York University, The Guggenheim Museum, The Hirshhorn Museum & The Albright-Knox Art Gallery. His paintings, drawings and collages have been published in many on line and print magazines. He has received three National Endowments For The Arts Fellowship, two Pollock-Krasner grants and The Adolph Gottlieb Foundation grant. Currently he teaches art at the United Federation of Teachers Retiree Program in Brooklyn http://s110.photobucket.com/albums/n94/irajoel/artwork/

MICHAEL HAEFLINGER is originally from Dayton, OH. His work has appeared at Maverick, BlazeVOX, milk, and in the tall-lighthouse anthology, city lighthouse. He lives in Berlin, Germany.

HEATHER HALDEMAN lives in Pasadena, California and began writing professionally nine years ago. Her essays been published in *The Christian Science Monitor, Chicken Soup for the Soul, From Freckles to Wrinkles, Grandmother Earth* and numerous online journals. She has received first, second and third place awards for her essays and is currently writing a book.

MONICA A HAND is a mother, grandmother, writer, book artist and poet. Her poetry can be found in *Black Renaissance Noire, Aunt Chloe, Naugatuck River Review,* E. Ethelbert Miller's *Beyond the Frontier,* Cave Canem's *Gathering Ground* and online in the Beltway Quarterly.

EMILY HAYES has an MA in English literature from Southern Illinois University, Carbondale. She teaches English at Carbondale Community High School and is the co-editor of *The Village Pariah*, a new literary journal sponsored by the Mark Twain Boyhood Home and Museum. Her works have previously appeared or are forthcoming in *The Mom Egg, Paterson Literary Review, Diverse Voices Quarterly, InkSpotter, Big Lucks, Bayonet,* and *New Scriptor.* She is known as Mama to her four-year-old son, Benjamin, a little boy who already understands the power of poems.

LYNN HOFFMAN is the author of *The Short Course in Beer* and *The New Short Course in Wine,* and the novel, *Bang BANG.* He was born in Brooklyn and lives in Philadelphia. A few years ago, he started writing poetry. His poetry has appeared in *Angelic Dynamo, Melusine, Waterways, Abramelin, The Broad Street Review* and *Short, Fast and Deadly.*

ANGELA HOOPER is an Oklahoman born and raised. Her only child, a daughter, was born to her when she was 44 years old. She feels extremely blessed and has found her to be an inspiration for her work. Her poetry was published in *The Crosstimbers*, a journal published by the University of Science and Arts of Oklahoma.

KELLI STEVENS KANE's poetry has appeared in *Spider Magazine* and *Denver Syntax*, and is forthcoming in *Word Riot* and *Mythium Literary Journal.* She is the recipient of a Serpent Source Foundation grant for an oral history work in progress about the Hill District of Pittsburgh. She was a selected participant in the 2009 VONA (Voices of Our Nations Arts Foundation) workshop for writers of color, "Building a Poetry Collection," taught by Willie Perdomo. Her first poetry manuscript is currently making the rounds in multiple first book contests. For more info visit www.planetsaturday.com/kelli.

DONNA KATZIN is Executive Director of Shared Interest, a non-profit investment fund that advances equitable development in South Africa's communities of color. Her poetry is informed by he work, her family and struggles for social justice.
Poet/performer PENN KEMP has published 25 books of poetry and drama, ten CDs and six videopoems: www.myspace.com/pennkemp/; http://www.mytown.ca/pennkemp/. She is University of Western Ontario's writer-in-residence. The League of Poets proclaimed Penn a foremother of Canadian poetry. http://mytown.ca/poemforpeace/ includes many translations of her poem.

klipschutz is the pen name of Kurt Lipschutz, a long-time resident of San Francisco; his books are *Twilight of the Male Ego* (2002), *The Good Neighbor Policy* (1989) and *The Erection of Scaffolding for the Re-Painting of Heaven by the Lowest Bidder* (1985, o.p). He is the publisher of the limited edition collectible *ALL ROADS. . .But This One* (Luddite Kingdom Press, 2006). His work has been in anthologies and magazines, e.g. *Poetry* (of Chicago) and *Ambit* (U.K.). He is also a songwriter, with Chuck Prophet, Bone Cootes and others.

CYNTHIA KRAMAN's new poetry collection is *The Touch* (Bowery Books 2009),nominated for the Kingsley Tufts Award and The Poetry Society of America's William Carlos Williams Award. ³My Own Private Iditarod² was nominated for a Pushcart Prize. "Promised Land", her play set in the aftermath of 9-11, previewed at the Algonquin Theatre in October. Cynthia was lead singer/songwriter for the Seattle punk band CHINAS COMIDAS whose live and studio recordings were released in 2006 on Exquisite Corpse Records.

MINDY KRONENBERG teaches writing and literature at SUNY Empire State College, and has published poetry and prose in numerous literary journals and anthologies, including *The Southampton Review*, *Confrontation*, and *The Saint Ann's Review*. She edits *Book/Mark Quarterly Review*, and authored a chapbook of poems, *Dismantling the Playground*.

A working actor, DINAH LENNEY has written for numerous journals, and is the author of *Bigger than Life: A Murder, a Memoir*, excerpted in *The New York Times*. She currently teaches in the Master of Professional Writing program at the University of Southern California, in the Bennington Writing Seminars, and for the Rainier Writing Workshop at Pacific Lutheran University. Dinah lives in Los Angeles with her husband and two children.

VERONICA LIU's writing and visual art have appeared in *Broken Pencil*, *Quick Fiction*, *Pax Americana*, *We'll Never Have Paris*, *Get Ahead*, and other journals and zines. In 2010 she is the recipient of a Northern Manhattan Arts Alliance grant to support the completion of her first novel, and a Manhattan Community Arts Fund grant to coordinate an uptown arts festival. She is cofounder of the publishing collective Fractious Press and the online community radio station Washington Heights Free Radio.

TARA L. MASIH is editor of the acclaimed *Rose Metal Press Field Guide to Writing Flash Fiction* (2009) and author of *Where the Dog Star Never Glows: Stories* (Press 53, 2010). She has published fiction, poetry, and essays in numerous anthologies and literary magazines (including *Confrontation*, *Hayden's Ferry Review*, *Natural Bridge*, *Flash*, *Night Train*, and *The Caribbean Writer*). Several limited edition illustrated chapbooks featuring her flash fiction have been published by The Feral Press. She received first place in *The Ledge Magazine*'s fiction contest, and Pushcart Prize, Best New American Voices, and Best of the Web nominations. www. taramasih.com. "Catalpa" © by Tara L. Masih, from *Where the Dog Star Never Glows*, originally appeared in *Fragile Skins*.

JOAN MAZZA has worked as a medical microbiologist, psychotherapist, certified sex therapist, writing coach and seminar leader. She is the author of six books, *including Dreaming Your Real Self* (Perigee/Penguin). Her work has appeared in *Potomac Review*, *Möbius*, *Pennsylvania English*, *Writer's Digest Magazine*, *Playgirl*, *The Writer*, and *Writer's Journal*. She now writes poetry and does fabric art in rural central Virginia. www.JoanMazza.com

HEATHER MCALLISTER, full time mother of Clayton 10 and Jake almost 2, is an actress, director and writer jumping back into the working world after her baby break. Her NY theatre reviews can be found here: http://www.nytheatre.com/nytheatre/reviewerinfo.php?rev=16

KIM MCMECHAN is a singer-songwriter and poet who lives in Kelowna, BC, Canada. She has won multiple awards for her songs, which, these days, are mostly about life with her two daughters, Iryn 7 and Ella 4. When songwriting time became a little more scarce two years ago (her daughters stopped napping and started drawing on the walls) Kim took up photography. This is her first published photo. www.kimmcmechan.com

COLLEEN MICHAELS teaches writing at Montserrat College of Art. Her poems and essays have appeared or are forthcoming in *Literary Mama*, *Bread and Circus*, and *Blue Collar Review*. She was a finalist in the Split This Rock 2010 poetry competition for her poem "Something Fragile." She has been commissioned by The Trustees of the Reservation to create a public art installation of her poem "Align" at Crane Beach in Ipswich, Massachusetts. She lives in Beverly, Massachusetts with her grounded husband and buoyant daughter.

MARY HARTER MITCHELL was a Professor with the Indiana University School of Law, Indianapolis. In addition teaching law and writing, Mary homeschooled both her daughters to high school and cared for her own mother who suffered from Parkinson's Disease. Although Mary passed away this November from breast cancer, she continues to inspire her many students and friends. Mary's poems have appeared in the *Journal of Legal Education* and the *Indianapolis Star*.

TEDDY NORRIS would like to live in a seaside villa and play the cello. In real life, she writes poetry in the Midwest where she lives with her husband and one geriatric cat, teaches creative writing at St. Charles Community College, and edits the college literary journal, *Mid Rivers Review*.

SANDRA RAMOS O'BRIANT's work has appeared in *LiteraryMama, Whistling Shade, Flashquake, Café Irreal. La Herencia, latinola.com*, and *The Copperfield Review*. In addition, her short stories have been anthologized in *Best Lesbian Love Stories of 2004, What Wildness is This: Women Write About the Southwest* (University of Texas Press, Spring 2007), *Latinos in Lotus Land: An Anthology of Contemporary Southern California Literature,* (Bilingual Press, 2008), and *Hit List: The Best of Latino Mystery* (Arte Publico, 2009). Visit her at www.bloodmother.com

JUDITH O'BRIEN has had three volumes of her poetry published: *Everything That Is, Is Connected,* Village Books Press, 2007, *By the Grace of Ghosts,* co-authored with Jane Taylor, Village Books Press, 2005, and *Mythic Places,* ByLine Press, 2000, *Crossing a Different Bridge: an Oklahoma Memoir* will be published late Spring of this year, 2010 by Mongrel Empire Press.

THETA PAVIS is a poet, journalist and editor. Her work has been widely published in journals and magazines. She's been honored twice by the Society of Professional Journalists. She blogs about parenting for the New Jersey Moms Blog and on her blog North Jersey Beanstalk: www. beanstalknj.blogspot.com/. She is the founder of Ink Stained Mothers, a network for moms who write.

PUMA PERL's poetry and fiction have been published in over 100 print and online journals and anthologies. Her first chapbook, *Belinda and Her Friends*, published in 2008, was awarded the Erbacce Press 2009 Poetry Award in a field of over 1400 applicants; a full-length collection, *knuckle tattoos,* was published in early 2010. She performs her work in many venues, in and out of New York City. She lives and writes on the Lower East Side and has facilitated writing workshops in community based agencies and at Riker's Island, a NYC prison. She believes in the transformative and healing power of the arts. http://pumaperl.blogspot.com/

MARCIA POPP is a retired university professor and the author of several textbooks and biographies. Her first book of poetry, comfort in small rooms, was published in 2009, and the title poem won the Robert G. Cohn Prose Poetry Award for 2008. "strike up the band" from the collection was included in Best New Poets 2008, edited by Mark Strand. Other poetry has appeared in *Memoir (and)* and *Avocet: A Journal of Nature Poems.*

KYLE POTVIN's poetry has appeared in print and online publications including *The Lyric, The Mom Egg,* JAMA (Journal of the American Medical Association), *Literary Mama, The Barefoot Muse, Measure, The New York Times* "Well" blog and *The 2008 & 2010 Poets' Guide to New Hampshire.* She was named a finalist for the 2008 Howard Nemerov Sonnet Award. She is principal of a public relations firm and mother to two boys, 8 & 10.

Recent poetry by TANIA PRYPUTNIEWICZ appeared either in print or on-line at *Autumn Sky, Literary Mama, Linebreak, Salome Magazine,* and *Tiny Lights*; new poems are forthcoming at *The Blood Orange Review.* A graduate of the Iowa Writers' Workshop, she is the poetry editor at the *Fertile Source* (www.fertilesource.com). She lives in Sonoma County, California with her husband, three children, and five feral cats and keeps a blog documenting the process of mothering while writing at Feral Mom, Feral Writer (www.poetrymom.blogspot.com).

JESSY RANDALL'S young adult novel *The Wandora Unit* (Ghost Road Press, 2009) is about love and friendship in the high school literary crowd. Her collection of poems *A Day in Boyland* (Ghost Road Press, 2007) was a finalist for the Colorado Book Award. Her website is http:// personalwebs.coloradocollege.edu/~jrandall.

CHARLES P. RIES lives in Milwaukee, Wisconsin. His narrative poems, short stories, interviews, and poetry reviews have appeared in over two hundred print and electronic publications. He has received four Pushcart Prize nominations for his writing. Most recently he was interviewed by Jane Crown for Blog Radio. www.janecrown.com . You may find additional samples of his work by going to: http://www.literati.net/Ries/. He is a founding member of the Lake Shore Surf Club, the oldest fresh water surfing club on the Great Lakes and the proud father-mother of Isabel and Catherine.

ELLEN RIX is a mom, wife, artist, gardener and very happy with life!

HELEN RUGGIERI spent some time in Japan recently researching a 13th century trip by a 57 year old Buddhist nun who traveled from Kyoto to Kamakura and kept a record in her "Journal of the Waning Moon." The video is on Ruggieri's website www.HelenRuggieri.com

ELLEN SAUNDERS' poems have appeared in *Prairie Schooner, Poetry East, Calyx Journal, Pearl, Toronto Review, Boston Literary Review, The Lyric*, and *The Mom Egg*, among several others.

LEE SCHWARTZ is a wife and mother whose daughter is a freshman at Smith College. She has won Honorable Mention 2008 and Editor's Choice 2009 Allen Ginsberg Awards in the Paterson Literary Journal. She has published in The Mom Egg print and online Journal since 2007. She is included in the Seed6 Journal from Hidden Book Press. Her work appears online in Protestpoems.org, 2009. She has been an Artist in Residence at the 92nd St Y. Catch her reading at The Bowery Poetry Club and Cornelia Street Café in her own Greenwich Village locale.

ELIZABETH SCHWYZER has worked as a freelance writer and arts journalist in the UK and the states since 2002. She is currently an arts editor and writer for the *Santa Barbara Independent*. She has also worked as a professional dancer and choreographer, yoga and martial arts instructor, and outdoor guide. When she's not writing, you can find her dancing, mentoring teenagers, riding her powder blue Vespa, snowboarding, hiking, and training for a triathlon and for a second degree black belt in Dynamic Circle Hapkido. http://www.independent.com/elizabethschwyzer

MARGUERITE SCOTT teaches composition and poetry at The College of Charleston. She earned her Ph.D. in Creative Writing from The Florida State University and her work has appeared in *Feminist Studies* and *The Evansville Review* among others. Aside from these career facts, her days are spent, mostly, jotting down new surprises on scratch pieces of paper, changing diapers, and laughing at the absurdities of love intersecting with stress.

LYNNE SHAPIRO is a writer and teacher who lives in Hoboken, New Jersey with her husband and son. She's had poems and essays published in *Mslexia, Terrain.org, Umbrella, Quay,* and *Qarrtsiluni*. Her work has been included in *Eating Her Wedding Dress: A Collection of Clothing Poems* (Ragged Sky Press), *Pain and Memory* (Editions Bibliotekos) and *Decomposition, An Anthology of Fungi-Inspired Poems* (Lost Horse Press).

MARIAN KAPLUN SHAPIRO, a previous contributor, practices as a psychologist and poet in Lexington, Massachusetts. She is the author of a professional book, *Second Childhood* (Norton, 1988), a poetry book, *Players In The Dream, Dreamers In The Play* (Plain View Press, 2007) and two chapbooks: *Your Third Wish*, (Finishing Line, 2007); and *The End Of The World, Announced On Wednesday* (Pudding House, 2007). She was named Senior Poet Laureate of Massachusetts in 2006 and again in 2008.

CAROLEE SHERWOOD's poetry has been published or is forthcoming in *Pirene's Fountain, Awakenings Review, Wicked Alice, Qarrtsiluni, Glass: A Journal of Poetry* and *Ballard Street Poetry Journal* (which nominated her poem "How to Let Wild Birds Out" for a Pushcart Prize in 2008). For three years, she was part of the creative team that produced Read Write Poem. She co-edits *Ouroboros Review* and writes reviews for *Poets' Quarterly*.

ANA SILVA is a new mother of twin girls, now 2, who writes poetry and teaches English at The Spence School in New York City. She has an MA in Philosophy and one in English. She says, "The moment I became pregnant was the moment my relationship with my own mother became more difficult. I'm still trying to figure out why. These poems are part of my attempt to understand my mother, myself."

AMANDA SKJEVELAND'S work has recently appeared in *Melusine, Eclipse, Flutter Poetry Journal, Burst, Literary Mama, The Write Room,* and *Tonopah Review*. She lives with her husband and two little boys on the east coast, where she teaches English and edits the literary magazine at a community college.

GOLDA SOLOMON, poet, professor , parent and grand-parent is the host of Po'Jazz (Poetry in Partnership with Jazz) in residence several Third Thursdays at The Cornelia Street Café. Solomon also gigs around the city and goes on the road with a fabulous roster of jazz musicians. Her words may be found in anthologies, e-zines, journals and CD's. Her work is in previous *Mom Eggs* and she is currently preparing a manuscript for publication. She is a member of WOMENWRITE, nyc and Word of Mouth writers. Solomon is also a proud poetry outreach mentor for CCNY and the annual City College Poetry Festival. She was recently appointed poet-in-residence at The Blue Door Gallery, Yonkers, New York where she facilitates ArtSpeak , ekphrastic creative writing workshops.(partially funded by Poets and Writers). www.jazzjaunts.com, contact gs@goldajazz.com.

DR. ROXANNE SUKOL is a physician and writer in Cleveland, Ohio. She is a 2008 winner of the Baltimore Review's Creative Nonfiction Contest (2nd place) for her essay "Redefined Wheat." She blogs on real food and nutrition at "Your Health is on Your Plate."

KATHERINE SWETT is a native of New York City where she lives with her husband and three children. In addition to writing poetry, she is chairman of the English department in an independent K-12 school.

SUSAN TEPPER'S collection *Deer & Other Stories* is just out from Wilderness House Press. She has received five Pushcart Prize Nominations for fiction and poetry, and her stories have appeared/forthcoming in *Green Mountains Review, American Letters & Commentary, Gargoyle, Crannog* (Ireland), *WOW!* (Ireland), *Schuylkill Valley Journal, Sundaysalon.com,* Cervena Barva Press and elsewhere. She curates FIZZ a reading series at KGB Bar in NYC, and is Assistant Editor of the Istanbul Literary Review (online journal based in Turkey).

FLORA TREBI-OLLENNU holds an MA in Geography from the University of Saskatchewan and BSc (Hons) in Planning from the University of Science and Technology, Ghana. She has authored five books for young adults, including *My Daily Walk: Discover the Life of Jesus,* the second in the *My Daily Walk* series, which will roll out in 2010. In addition to homeschooling one of her four children, she also reads regularly in various elementary schools, and has been featured as a main speaker in church related events.

HEATHER TRUETT is a young mom, writer and minister's wife living in the birthplace of Elvis, Tupelo MS. She teaches poetry and creative writing, does a lot of laundry and reads way more than is emotionally healthy. http://www.madamerubies.com/

DONNA VORREYER lives in the Chicago area where she is both a middle school teacher and a mom. Her work has been published in numerous journals including *Cider Press Review, Literary Mama, New York Quarterly, Autumn Sky Poetry, Boxcar Poetry Review,* and *Ghoti.* Her chapbook *Womb/Seed/Fruit,* which chronicles her journey to motherhood through infertility and adoption, will be published by Finishing Line Press in June 2010. http://www.donnavorreyer.com/

AMY WATKINS' poems have recently appeared in *The Louisville Review, Literary Mama* and *Conclave: A Journal of Character.* She lives in Orlando with her husband and daughter. The best thing she learned from her mother is that whatever you are most self-conscious about "will never be seen on a galloping horse."

LISA WILLIAMS is the author of the memoir, *Letters to Virginia Woolf,* published by Hamilton Books (June 2005), www.letterstovirginiawoolf.com. She also wrote, *The Artist as Outsider in the Novels of Toni Morrison and Virginia Woolf* (Greenwood Press, 2000). Lisa's work has appeared in such publications as *The Mom Egg, The Women's Studies Quarterly, The*

Tusculum Review, The Virginia Woolf Miscellany, and *For She is the Tree of Life: Grandmothers Through the Eyes of Women Writers*. She teaches writing and literature at Ramapo College of New Jersey.

KRIS WOLL has lived and worked in New England, New York City, and now Minneapolis since leaving her prairie hometown. She has a MA in history and is interested the pasts we've lived, inherited, and imagined. She is a 2009 mnartists.org mnLit miniStories Grand Prize Winner, and her work has appeared in *Minnesota, MinnPost, Prairie Poetry, Edible Twin Cities* and (forthcoming) *Memoir (and)*. Read her blog at http://alittlepractice.blogspot.com/.

CATHERINE WOODARD lives and plays basketball in NYC, was a journalist and president of Artists Space and is part of the Poetry Society of America's Centennial cabal. More poems about a Southern family miming Egyptian death rituals are or will be in *Poet Lore, RHINO, Podium and RiverSedge*. Woodard is curating SeePoemsHear (.org online) and working to return Poetry in Motion to the NYC subways.

JOANNE G. YOSHIDA is a visual artist and poet who lives in Oita, Japan with her husband and daughter. Her most recent design project is a line of Yoga Mats to inspire peace and tranquility based on the Japanese character meaning "Stop". She chronicles her daily life and things she finds on http://aikawarazulifeinjapan.blogspot.com and http://foundinjapanjgy.blogspot.com.

KIRSTIN HOTELLING ZONA's poems have appeared or are forthcoming in a number of magazines, such as *The Southwest Review, Beloit Poetry Journal, Poet Lore, The Spoon River Poetry Review*, and *Literary Mama*. She is also the author of *Marianne Moore, Elizabeth Bishop, and May Swenson: The Feminist Poetics of Self-Restraint* (2002, Michigan UP), and Editor of *The Spoon River Poetry Review*. Kirstin lives with her family in Maine and Illinois, where she co-hosts *Poetry Radio* (WGLT 98.1) and is an associate professor at Illinois State University.

Made in the USA
Charleston, SC
16 April 2010